ACCOUNTING REVOLUTION

By Lynda Steffens

First published in 2019

PrintPublish Pty Ltd
1300 98 94 91 info@printpublish.com.au
Design and layout by Leanne Thompson, PrintPublish

Printed in Australia.

National Library of Australia Cataloguing-in-Publication entry:
ISBN 978-0-6486963-0-8

Testimonials

Thank goodness for Lynda and her passion for business. I've engaged a number of business coaches over the years, but nothing has revolutionised my business like Lynda's program has. If all accountants did this, the world would be a much better place for us small business owners. Accountants, get on board, you'd be crazy not to.

— Nik Cree, Owner, Positive Business Online.

From the way that Lynda communicates, it is easy to see that she is passionate about the accounting industry. It is Lynda's passion, paired with her practical experience in the industry, which resonates and will make this book one for the collection.

— Brendan Corino, Accountant, Fay and Redman.

Lynda is absolutely passionate about what she does and has such an incredible knowledge of the accounting industry. Lynda has changed my life. This book will change yours.

— Jeannie Anderson, Partner, Mayberry Meldrum Anderson.

Lynda is such a buzz to be around. Her experience within the accounting industry is evident in her knowledge of what a current accounting practice should be run like. She is passionate about passing on this knowledge to fellow accountants. I am looking forward to getting my hands on her new book as a motivator for myself. You should get one too.

— Robert Hills, Founder, The Exit Accountant.

Lynda's accounting industry knowledge is highly regarded and respected by those in the profession. Her ability to see through the issues being experienced and provide clarity on challenges faced in our industry is insightful, refreshing and very much appreciated. Lynda is truly a gift to the industry.

— Sonia O'Donnell, Director, Contego Accounting.

Finally, someone is delivering the HOW for accountants. We've heard all about the why and the what but that doesn't help with just getting on with it, refreshing!

— Greet Recoules, Owner, GreetYourBrand.com.

Business owners want and expect more from their accountants. Numbers aren't inanimate; they tell a story and good or bad, clients want to hear that story from their accountant. Lynda Steffens knows how to take you to that place where you have the time and the know-how to engage your clients with the story. Read this book carefully, then call Lynda and engage her services

— James Yuille, Owner, Mediaglue.

It has been an absolute pleasure working with Lynda. Her positivity and drive towards business success is infectious. I have personally switched to a new accountant who has worked with Lynda as I have seen first-hand the benefits which her program offers small business owners. I'm so happy I now have an accountant who provides coaching and is dedicated to the success of my business

— Cheryl Ambler, Owner, C & CO Marketing.

When you read this book you are learning from one of the best in the industry. With understanding, patience, good humour, and honesty, Lynda is incredibly passionate about sharing her expertise and knowledge with fellow accountants and systematically revolutionising the accounting industry through her proven methodology

— Pip Meecham, Founder ProjectBox.

CONTENTS

Dedication

To my mother and father for teaching me that determination and resilience are calm, confidence is quiet, and doing the right thing will never go out of fashion.

What is Accounting Revolution?

As an accountant, and an introvert, I've written this book for other motivated accountants. You're keen to learn, to do better for your clients. You're seeking a different way to connect with your clients, a way that expresses the true value of what you do.

Let's address the elephant in the room, shall we? We live in a world that looks up to extroverts. Communicating the value of what we do by changing our conversations sounds a lot like selling. Sales is the domain of the extrovert, and accountants for the most part are introverts. Accountants can't sell, in fact we stink at it. We stink at it because we're trying to use methods developed and taught by extroverts! To top it all off, when we fail, it reinforces the idea that we can't sell and that we should just give up.

NO, you absolutely, categorically, can't give up!

Let's be realistic. We're not going to succeed using sales processes developed by extroverts. That's all sales is, a process. All it takes to change our conversations is to follow a process, a process developed and written by an introvert – me!

I was sick and tired of seeing my friends, clients, colleagues, and my industry struggle with communicating the value of our services to clients and the resulting stress and pain driving amazing professionals from the industry. I had to find some way to help. I know the incredible value an accountant brings to a business and the untapped potential in that value, but clients don't. Why?

In short, we need to change our conversations.

I've dedicated the last 10 or so years to finding out what makes accountants tick, how we learn, how we adapt, what our strengths and weaknesses are. It's been a wild ride and a massive learning and personal development journey.

Most of us drawn to the accounting industry have a distinctive profile:

- We love information and detail. We're like the squirrel in *Ice Age* who covets the acorn. Information is our acorn of choice. We seek it out, collect it, hoard it – the more detailed, the better.

- We love using systems and processes to analyse this information, make sense of it, and keep it in check. With the massive amounts we collect, we'd be in real trouble if we had no way of organising it.

- We tend to be risk averse and of the mindset that if it ain't broke, don't fix it. We're not fans of change. No human is, but we're certainly on the lower end of the spectrum when it comes to adapting to change. This makes us measured and conservative in how we think and act, exactly what business owners want and look for in a financial advisor. They know we're not going to lose our heads over the latest fad.

- Amazingly, we have the ability to solve complex problems in our minds. This is one of our superpowers. I bet you've often felt you're three steps ahead of someone in understanding a concept or explaining something – that's our superpower minds at work. We're totally solution-focused and when left to our own devices we find it very difficult to be any other way. Therein lies one of our biggest issues. Solutions don't equate to an expression of value. We don't explain why, we just provide the solution.

Instinctively, this is who we are. It's in our DNA, the markers of who we really are, the Real Accountant. And it's all these traits, and more, that make us absolutely perfect for the job we do. BUT … you knew there'd be a but, didn't you … we can't do our jobs in the best possible way unless we connect with our clients in a way that communicates our value. A way the clients can understand, so they see the value in what we do and want to work with us.

That's what this book is all about.

How to Get the Most out of this Book

Here are some tips.

Accountants love structure. So do I, so the book has a pretty solid structure.

This is a how-to book and I haven't held anything back. The detail is extensive, so you will find headings and sub-sections within the chapters to make it easy to locate the detail you need.

Three of the chapters are huge – Chapter 3 Time to DISCOVER, Chapter 4 Time to DIG and Chapter 8 The Master PLAN. These chapters cover the most implementation detail, and if you do any of my three-day workshops we dedicate more than half a day to learning and practising the techniques within each of these chapters. I recommend you don't skim-read them and expect to implement the processes. I know you're a skim-reader because I am too. It won't work. All the chapters are important but these three are vital to the process. You will need to read them thoroughly and most likely a number of times.

The Coach Approach

The book covers the essence of my three-phase program 'The Small Business Project', which combines the power of accounting and the best of coaching into one powerful modality. Throughout the book, I've highlighted the best bits of coaching – which I refer to as **The Coach Approach** – so you don't miss them or skim over them. These parts will help you revolutionise the way you engage with clients, so keep an eye out for them.

Rinse & Repeat

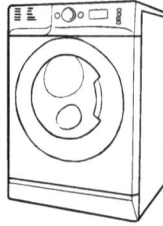

Sometimes, the only way something cements itself in our understanding is to read it, read it again, read it another seven times, then hear it, hear it another time, and on the third time, usually from another person, we might have an epiphany, an aha moment. Epiphany is one my favourite words, I think because it's the realisation that change is necessary. Besides, it sounds super-cool. Epiphany. I challenge you to use it in a sentence today. See how you go!

There are concepts in the book that will be foreign to you. Very few people have written sales processes with introverts in mind, and certainly no-one has written a sales process specifically with introverted accountants in mind. I recognise it's difficult to change, particularly due to our profile, and that it will take effort, time, and resources, both personally and professionally, but it's worth it.

Tricks of the Trade

We learn by making mistakes, so I've made sure to share mine with you. When I was formulating The Small Business Project program, I was also learning, working by trial and error and making plenty of mistakes. My **Tricks of the Trade** will allow you to fast-track and avoid some of them.

Actions and Additional Resources

The actions at the end of each chapter are designed to help you implement the processes you'll be reading about. They're short, sharp, and most take only 5–10 minutes each. They pack a punch when it comes to implementing The Small Business Project.

The book is also bursting with free additional resources. By purchasing the book, you have access to all the bonus material on my website: https://lyndasteffens.com/bonuses The first time you click on the link you'll need to nominate a user name and password. After that you can just log in at your leisure.

When writing this book, I was very happy and motivated and I know this shines through. I am happy to share The Small Business Project with you. Expect it to challenge norms, test your boundaries, and confront your pre-conceptions. There's no magic pill for change but 'through change comes freedom', so hang in there and enjoy the ride. Hold onto your hat … here we go!

Lynda Steffens

1

Sex Lies and Revolution

Truth is not what you want it to be. It is what it is, and you must bend to its power or live a lie

— *Miyamoto Musashi*[1]

---

1 Musashi and Harris, 2004

We've been kidding ourselves if we think we've been doing the best job possible by our clients, but the biggest calamity with all our industry posturing and lies is that we've let ourselves down. We've forgotten why we wanted to be accountants, and why we started out doing what we do. I believe business should be profitable, rewarding, and fun – even accounting. Otherwise, why do it at all? There is a hell of a lot of risk involved, both financially and emotionally. Don't get me wrong, we've been doing a great job, and a necessary and important one, but let's find our passion and motivation again because I believe we can do better.

I'm here to help you do just that.

Do more of the work you love. Think about the days you bounce into work. You know, those days you have the interesting jobs to do, the ones you can really sink your teeth into. Think about doing more of them.

Earn more money from clients who value what you do and will happily pay you for it. Yes, those clients exist, and you probably have some of them already. Imagine a business where you worked with these clients every single day doing work you love. Wouldn't it be amazing to go to work knowing that you attract clients you want to work with, doing the work you want to do, not just clients using your services because they have to for their tax returns and financials to stay compliant?

And what about your team? If you're happy and engaged, working with clients who value what you do and doing work you love, your team will also be happy and engaged. Employees can cause a lot of stress for business owners, and daily struggles and time spent managing people and your team can get you right off track. Imagine if your team was happy and engaged and they bounced into work just like you, doing the work they love with the clients they enjoy working with. With all the new clients you're attracting, the team have amazing opportunities to learn and to grow as professionals. A happy and engaged team is the dream.

Have a great work–life balance and reduce your stress. Many accountants I talk to are stressed because they work very hard, and often long hours, and do not have the balance they would like for spending time with their partners, families, and friends.

Future-proof your business. Changing your conversations is the key to delivering advisory services consistently, which in turn means growth and success for your business. You'll be doing the best job possible for your clients.

A recent *Accounting Today* survey reported that the two biggest concerns for the accounting industry today are the impact of technology and accountants' ability to adapt to the rapid pace of change and remain relevant. How are you going to remain relevant?

> *The secret of change is to focus all of your energy not on fighting the old but on building the new*
> — *Socrates*[2]

If you don't change the way you do business, you will be forced to continue with clients who do not value your work, who question everything you do, and who try to negotiate fees. It's simply not a sustainable business model. You'll remain stressed, overworked, and underpaid, with little or no work–life balance.

None of this paints a picture of a profitable business, a rewarding one, or a business that is in any way fun. You can't continue to rely on compliance and be forced to compete on price because it will simply become too hard to stay in business.

Let me ask you a question. Do clients value your work?

Accountants have traditionally provided a functional service doing tax returns and financial statements. Clients seek you out because they have to: the regulatory authorities have made business

---

2   Hutyra, 2019

compliance too complicated for most business owners to look after it themselves. So you've had a captive market of clients making grudge purchases, and you've never had to worry about your customers' accounting experience. Your business has made money in spite of all this.

As an accountant, you've been labelled a trusted advisor, basically because you know numbers, how to report them, and how to make sure a business is financially compliant. Business owners who have a business or money question go to an accountant.

What we're now realising is that we have vastly underestimated the value of our trusted advisor position and we have failed dismally in leveraging it.

The world has changed, with big organisations muscling into the trusted advisor market. We're facing the commoditisation of compliance. Advances in technology have allowed the offshoring of work. The supposed efficiency gains in data processing are putting consistent downward pressure on pricing and eroding profit margins. Regulators are accessing more and more information directly from the source, bypassing the middleman, us, accountants.

We've been trying to compete on price, our once-robust profit margins are diminishing, our growth is flatlining, we're working longer and harder delivering services we don't necessarily enjoy, and our teams are becoming increasingly less engaged.

I believe the accounting industry is at a critical tipping point, a point that if we don't change the way we engage with our clients we run the very real risk of completely losing our relevancy. This tipping point is driven not only by the factors just mentioned but also by a major generational shift in our client bases: what our clients want and the value they seek from their accountant, an expert, or an advisor.

Let's just talk about the differences between an expert and an advisor for a second. An expert's job is to be right, to solve client's problems using technical and professional skill, and to take the responsibility away from the client until the job is done. An advisor's job, on the other hand, is to be helpful rather than right. They provide guidance and input to support the client's own thought and decision-making processes. The client retains control and responsibility.

Thinking about the tipping point and generational shift in our client bases again, baby boomers play by the rules, placing a higher value on work than on personal life. Because of that, they expect, accept, and value expert advice – i.e. experts – from the accounting profession. Gen-Xers, on the other hand, are more about work–life balance. They value independence more than any other generation does. They will tolerate an expert but what they really want and value is an advisor. Millennials want to work smarter, not harder, with technology. They have information at their fingertips and don't need or want experts. They value advisors and are not afraid to bypass accountants to get what they want.

This generational shift in accountants' client bases is significant but for the most part, it appears to have been ignored or overlooked by other industry commentators.

In any case, it's critical we take a look at this problem of clients not valuing our work now, because we are the best and most qualified resource for business advice and support – and it's slipping through our fingers. Quite a number of accountants I talk to are financially strained. Most are highly stressed and emotionally drained. The collective resource of business information and advice comprising the accounting industry and the people in it cannot be allowed to diminish further, to where business just becomes so hard for us that we don't want to do it anymore. The business world needs us, our communities need us, and our economies need us.

So, what's the solution?

The solution is that as accountants, we change from being just a functional service to a vital resource for business owners.

Advisory services on their own are not the answer. Changing our conversations is.

As accountants, we have so much to offer the business world. We are the best placed and most qualified professionals to support business owners. In the age of the entrepreneur, the gig economy, it has never been easier to set up and start a business. Yet 60% of businesses fail before they even reach five years old.

If I have my way, accountants will play a significant role in changing this statistic. We will be restored as the most prominent provider of advice to the business community, and vital to business success.

I want you to join the revolution. I'm extremely proud of the accounting industry and its people. By making some small changes, I know it will bring back your passion and motivation for business.

I'll share with you exactly how to go about it. But first, let's talk about something a little taboo – coaching!

Let's Talk About Coaching

When I'm writing a keynote speech, content for a blog or a workshop, and most certainly several times through this book, a particular sentence will often make a song pop into my head. I grew up in a musical family. My mother and brother played the piano and the organ, and I played piano and flute. There was always music somewhere. I love music. It relaxes me and helps me express what I'm feeling, as well as bringing out my quirky side. So when I first wrote the heading 'Let's Talk about Coaching' the song that popped into my head was *Let's Talk About Sex* by Salt-N-Pepa.

'Let's talk about sex, hm hm, let's talk about hm hm hm, let's talk about hm hm hm, let's talk about sex.'

I apologise if the song is now going around and around in your head. Well, I'm not sorry, it's a great song. I recommend you download or stream it, then turn it up loud!

In all seriousness, this song is a great analogy for what I want to talk about. Just like sex is a taboo subject for some, coaching or business coaching for accountants has most definitely been a taboo subject.

Let me tell you a story.

I started consulting after I'd owned my accounting practices and been a practice manager of a larger firm. I had recently moved to the beautiful Gold Coast in Queensland Australia, where I still live by the way.

I knew I had to build up my business networks to ensure my business would be a success. I joined a number of networking groups. One group in particular, as part of its accountability platform, required its members to sit down with the other members and have a one-to-one meeting to explain more about the business and understand how we could help each other through referrals. My fellow members would ask me, 'Lynda, what is it that you do?' My initial immediate response was, 'It's easier to tell you what I don't do, and what I'm not. I'm not a coach.'

I spent the first six to 12 months of my consulting career thinking that I wasn't a coach and avoiding it like the plague. I was reacting to coaching just as I had been conditioned by my industry to do. Coaching was a bad word and a taboo subject. After talking with a lot of my fellow networkers and other entrepreneurs and consulting with businesses, I realised what my business clients were seeing the most value in and gaining the most benefit from – the coaching techniques I was unwittingly using. They were also referring me to other business owners. My epiphany (see? I used it in a sentence) that I was coaching and that I am a coach was huge, and closely followed by the realisation that the combination of coaching methodologies, the power of my financial knowledge, and my business advice skills produced unbelievable results. My business clients were lapping it up because it was exactly what they were looking for.

Long story short, I stopped avoiding coaching and went about educating myself about coaching. I'm an accountant, I love information, information is power, and I've always enjoyed learning. The resulting professional and personal development journey that is ongoing was nothing short of enlightening.

My Key Learnings About Coaching

Coaching is not ...

It's easier to start with what coaching is not, because it helps bust some common myths about this taboo subject, making it taboo no more!

Coaching is not mentoring, coaching is not consulting, coaching is not training. It's not therapy, friendship, or doing.

Just like the proverb, 'Give a man a fish and he'll eat for a day, teach a man to fish and he'll eat for a lifetime', as a coach, you want to teach your client how to fish, not give them the fish. If you give your client the fish, they may keep returning because they need the fish and eventually, they will resent having to come back and it will be a grudge purchase.

Think tax and compliance. That's how these services work. You give your clients the fish. This is exactly as compliance should be, it wouldn't work any other way, but if you apply the same principles to business advice, it doesn't work. By teaching your client to fish, they are more likely to come back to you wanting to know more, how to fish better, what bait to use, what equipment is best, how to catch more fish, all excellent questions your advisory services will help them answer. Create the thirst for knowledge and clients will happily pay for the knowledge, advice, and answers. If you don't create the thirst for knowledge, you'll just be stuck selling fish.

Hmmm, coaching sounds a lot like an advisor, doesn't it?

Coaching Is ...

Coaching is a process. Yep, you read that correctly, a process. Processes have structure, and accountants love process and structure. Had an epiphany yet?

Coaching is a process that aims to improve performance by focusing on the here and now rather than on the distant past or the future.

A coach is not an expert but a facilitator of learning. A coach helps people move from where they are now to where they want to be. They stimulate a client's own self-discovery by asking powerful questions. Nothing taboo about asking powerful questions, is there? No. Except maybe our very real fear of not knowing the answer. Don't worry. I've got that covered too and we'll get to it. After reading this book you need never feel this fear again.

These basic methodologies and the process of coaching embody my engagement model, which will allow you to instantly connect with your clients. Am I trying to teach you to become a coach? Definitely not. There is a whole lot more to coaching than what I could tell you in just one book, but I am showing you how to use all the power of accounting and all the best bits of coaching to bring these two worlds together into one powerful modality.

I love this quote:

> *If I have seen further than others, it is by standing on the shoulders of giants*
>
> — *Isaac Newton*[3]

---

3   BrainyQuote, 2019

The Urban Legend that is Advisory

'Advisory' is just a word but as an industry, we've come to be completely and utterly discombobulated by it. Oh my goodness, I've used another of my favourite words. Discombobulated, to be confused and disconcerted. We're confused about what advisory means. We've hyped it up, we've complicated it and made it something to fear. This thing that is so integral to what we do has become a real challenge for us to implement. Believe me, there are plenty of suppliers in the market making a lot of money out of our fear and confusion.

Compounding the challenge to implement and deliver advisory services is that we've been trying to deliver them the same as we deliver compliance, as experts. It doesn't work.

Ask 100 different accountants what advisory means to them and you'll get 100 different answers! That's because it can be different for each of us. In its simplest form, the definition of advisory is everything that is not compliance.

The first thing you need to do is define what advisory means to you and your business.

Action!

Here's your first action item of the book … actually, no it's not. Streaming *Let's Talk about Sex* was. Are you still singing it?

Take a few minutes to make a list of all the advisory services you currently offer. Remember: advisory is anything that is not compliance.

Add to the list the starting price for each service item. The minimum you would charge a client is a good place to start, not what you should be charging. If the starting price is zero, write zero. You'll find out further in the book why accountants are so very, very good at giving away stuff.

The second (or third if you're counting the song) action item is to make a list of all the advisory services you'd like to offer, and what you think the starting prices for these services would be. To help you out with the starting prices, think about conducting the service in its simplest form, with no complexity and for a small uncomplicated entity.

Put these lists away for safekeeping. You'll use them again later as you work through the book.

The Real Accountant

As I touched on in the introduction, I believe it's in the DNA of those attracted to the accounting industry that they:

- Love information and detail

- Use systems and processes to organise and analyse

- Are measured and conservative in their approach

- Have a superpower ability to solve complex problems in their minds

- For the most part, are introverts.

Over the last 10 years or so of my 25+-year career in the accounting industry, I've devoted myself to understanding the Real Accountant. Since moving from practising accounting to practice management and then to consulting and coaching, my job has been to bring out the best in accountants, help them achieve, inspire them, and support them to be the best they can be.

To do my job, I needed to know what makes us tick and I couldn't just rely on my own drivers, profile, and experiences even though I'm an accountant too.

What I found is that the Real Accountant is the person who hides behind a professional image. We hide behind our tax facts, tax knowledge, and tax legislation because that makes us feel safe. Being an expert makes us feel safe because that mode of operation plays right into the hands of our accountant DNA.

Take a second to look back over the definitions of 'expert' and 'advisor' I used earlier in the chapter. Works, doesn't it? We've been conditioned to think that our value lies in pumping out work and in having all the answers. We've mistakenly thought that a lot of what we know is common knowledge and that it's of little value, hence why we are so good at giving away information for free. In fact, very little of what we know is common knowledge at all, and our unique skill set enables us to deliver key information and insight into the operations of any business.

It's likely you will have read sales books, or had some sales training, and are familiar with the principle of 'know, like, and trust'. People buy from those they know, like, and trust. As accountants, we've almost always had trust because of our financial knowledge, but we've not necessarily had the 'know' and the 'like', partly because we've been busy hiding behind our professional image and in being experts, drowning our clients in historical performance data and tax law.

It's time you found the Real Accountant. Here are some tips for getting started.

Tip: The Real Accountant

Never stop learning and growing as a person. It's key to your success and happiness. Embrace the Real Accountant.

Tip: Out of your Comfort Zone

Yes, this is new, yes, this is different, yes, it will be foreign to you and yes, it will take practice and effort.

This is a revolution. You wouldn't expect anything less, and as you're still reading, then you're looking for something new, a different way, and you're still up for the challenge.

Tip: Practise

Practise, practise, practise. Don't fool yourself into thinking you can do this without practice. I know you'll try, and probably more than once. You're extremely time conscious so you'll think, hang it, I'll wing it. I guarantee you won't get a great result if you take this approach. How do I know? Because I did this too! Role-play with a team member or a friend. Put in the time and you'll get a great result.

Oh my goodness, did she just tell me to role-play? Yes, yes I did. I know, I dislike role-playing with a passion too but hey, it works.

Tip: Speaking Aloud

Make sure you speak aloud when you practise. Don't just think about what you would say by running through it in your mind. While internal monologue is the accountant's go-to technique (we love to do things in our heads), it won't work for practising what to say. As an introvert, you'll struggle to produce the words when you need them if all you've done is think them through. The cat, the dog, or even the chair works well to practise on.

Let me introduce you to Jeannie. Jeannie is a director of an accounting firm. When I met Jeannie at a networking event a couple of years ago, she was pretty stressed. Her clients were demanding and difficult to deal with, the pricing of services was always a tussle, and motivating herself and her team was a struggle for her. She had lost the passion and motivation for what she did and sometimes found herself not even wanting to go to work. All Jeannie was focused on was finding the easiest and most successful way for her to spend the next five to 10 years before leaving the industry.

Fast forward 12 months of working together and Jeannie is reinvigorated and inspired to help family businesses achieve their goals. She wakes up every day happy to go to work. Her team is engaged and kicking some amazing production goals. Her turnover is up, the profitability of her team has improved, and she's loving work life again. Jeannie knows she's still got a little way to go to achieve a 10 out 10 rating for her business, but she can see the light at the end of the tunnel. She's still working towards her exit strategy but it's with an entirely new mindset and focus.

If you feel remotely like Jeannie, here are some key things that worked for her.

Tip: Keep Things Simple

Don't try to solve problems you don't have yet.

Tip: The Butterfly Effect

Small changes for big impact.

Tip: Just Start

It's natural to analyse everything and then analyse it again to be sure. Just start. It won't be perfect but you'll have started.

After reading everything in this chapter, you're probably thinking you know and understand there's a problem, but it looks like an awful lot of change, and you're way too busy to change things right now.

Just remember to take your time, gather the information you need, and the change will come easily. I will show you that it's not a lot of change, just small changes that will make big differences for you, your clients, and your business.

You might also be thinking that you already offer advisory services, and so why do you need to change anything?

Yes, most accountants do offer advisory services but from my experience, clients don't often use those services, certainly not in any consistent manner. Clients tend to only engage with advisory services in an ad hoc manner at best. With my engagement model, your whole team will have the ability to offer and provide advisory services consistently.

You might also think that your clients are happy, that they do value what you do because they always pay their bills.

Let me tell you a quick story about Michelle. Michelle is an up-and-coming lawyer. She had huge growth plans for her practice and wanted to get cracking with them, but was uncertain because of what she envisaged as the financial unknown and risks involved. Michelle and I knew each other quite well and she knew that I worked with accountants, so of course we got to talking about her accountants. As it turned out, I knew her accountants and had spoken to them about their business. They believed their clients were happy. They always gave their clients the advice they wanted and in turn, their clients valued what they did and always paid their bills. They didn't need to change anything.

When I reiterated this to Michelle, she looked at me in absolute horror. She said, 'No Lynda, from my perspective that's not what's happening. In fact, I'm looking for another accountant because they're not giving me the advice I want. Actually, they just don't seem to care. I don't know how to ask them for what I need, they don't seem interested and just talk about what they want to talk about.'

You can see just from Michelle's story that we cannot afford to be complacent. We might think our clients are happy and that they value what we do because they pay their bills, but they may not be. They're looking for something else.

I guarantee the effort is worth it. The Small Business Project works. Clients will value the changes and the work you do and respect you for doing it.

So, let's roll our sleeves up and go to work.

Actions to Take After Reading This Chapter

1. Download and play *Let's Talk About Sex* by Salt-N-Pepa ☺

2. List all the advisory services you currently offer and the starting price you're currently charging for each service.

3. List all the advisory services you would like to offer and a starting price for each service.

2

Business Metamorphosis®

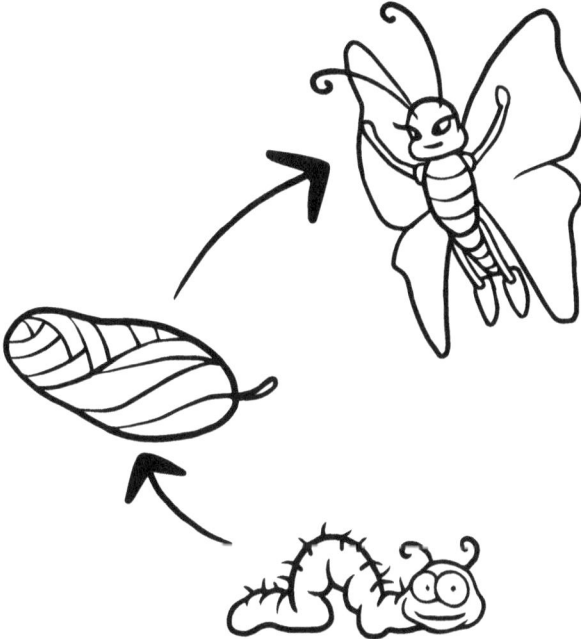

Metamorphosis is the most profound of all acts
— *Catherynne M Valente*[4]

---

4   Valente, 2006

The Business Metamorphosis® model is a simple, structured, high-level informational grid depicting the life cycle of a business. It is the foundation of my client engagement model, and phase one of The Small Business Project.

Business Metamorphosis® is made up of two parts:

1. The model

2. The process.

In this chapter, I unpack the **model** and explain how to introduce it to clients.

The Business Metamorphosis® **process** encompasses the 3Ds: DISCOVER, DIG, and DELIVER. Chapters 3, 4, and 5 explore the Business Metamorphosis® process and the 3Ds.

From here on, let's call it the BM model, or BM, to make it easier.

The BM model is simple and successful. It takes the stress out of business advisory conversations and removes the fear of not being able to answer client questions. It gives you all the information and structure you need so you don't have to think on the spot when chatting to your clients about their business.

> *Simplicity is the ultimate sophistication*
> — *Leonardo da Vinci*[5]

Not being able to answer client questions is, funnily enough, one of our greatest fears. This fear often stops us from venturing outside our expert mindset, which works perfectly for compliance-driven conversations but not for business advisory discussions.

Fear no more, the BM model expertly guides and directs your business advice conversations to help you pinpoint your questions

---

5   https://www.leonardodavinci.net, 2019

and answers. Discussions will no longer stall. You'll keep right on track, and have precious seconds to formulate all the questions and answers you will need.

Making the transition from expert to advisor is easy when you stop setting yourself up to fail by trying to deliver advisory services using an expert mindset. The BM model plays right into your information-gathering instincts, keeping you centred and focused on the questions you need to ask clients to gather the information necessary to leverage into advisory services. You'll feel secure in the knowledge that whatever pops up in a client discussion, you'll be prompted to ask the right question, and give exactly the right answer.

Once you have the freedom to relax, you can listen to and engage with your clients in a way you've only ever dreamed of. Listening to what your client has to say rather than focusing on formulating the next question or answer in your mind is a much better use of your time and ability. You can kick to the curb the responsibility of being an expert, of having to be right, and connect with your clients as a business owner and advisor rather than as an expert.

In just 10 minutes, you'll help clients identify, and bridge, the gap of where they are now in their business journey and where they want to be in the future. In your role of coach and advisor, you'll be using the key BM concept of 'now' and 'the future', helping your clients to move from where they are now to where they want to be in the future.

One in four business owners say their accountants have never sought feedback from them (NAB, 2018 'Key Insights into the Australian Accounting Industry').

Reliance on Compliance

If you continue to have the same client conversations, approaching advisory services with an expert mindset, you will continue to set yourself up to fail with advisory services, forcing an ongoing reliance on compliance.

You'll continue to compete on price, slicing into your profit margins more and more as inevitable improvements in technology and artificial intelligence affect the compliance market.

Clients will persist in undervaluing your work, business growth will be difficult, and the stress and financial rewards of business will diminish.

Doesn't sound like a whole lot of fun to me.

The Business Metamorphosis® Model

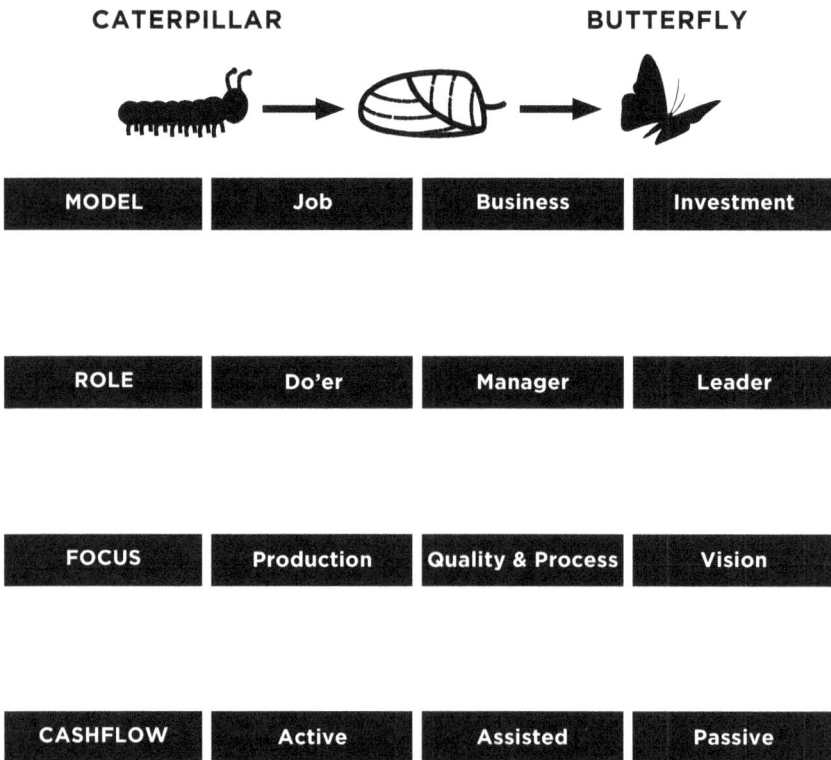

MODEL	Job	Business	Investment
ROLE	Do'er	Manager	Leader
FOCUS	Production	Quality & Process	Vision
CASHFLOW	Active	Assisted	Passive

Figure 2.1 The Business Metamorphosis® Model

The BM model is made up of three key stages – caterpillar, chrysalis, and butterfly across the top, and four key concepts down the left-hand side – model, role, focus, and cashflow.

There is no right or wrong with BM, and no-one likes to be told their business is wrong because it doesn't fit into a certain box or structure. Your client may initially indicate they are very happy at whatever stage they are currently at. BM allows this to be 100% acceptable. However, that's not to say because your client is happy with their stage, you can't have powerful conversations with them using the BM model. You most certainly can and in my experience, your client, after thinking about it for a little while, will likely want to talk with you further about how they can work their way through the relevant stages.

In any case, the BM model is very flexible and most certainly not linear. No business is that simple, particularly one in a growth phase. I'll explore that further after working through the stages and key concepts. Regardless of where your client identifies their business to sit within the BM model, you have the opportunity to work with them extensively in any phase.

Caterpillar

When a business is in the caterpillar stage, the BM model identifies the business owner as having a **JOB**. The business owner's role is that of a **DOER.** Don't you love my technical term? Just bear in mind I'm breaking down the need to be and act as an expert. There's a method in my madness, I promise. The business owner or owners do everything that the business requires. Their focus is wholly and solely on **PRODUCTION**, producing whatever it is that the business does and needs. The business owner is 100% **ACTIVE** in the generating of business cash flow. It's them and only them.

Chrysalis

In the chrysalis stage, the BM model indicates what most people associate with what a **BUSINESS** should look like. It is likely that employees, subcontractors, and consultants are helping the business owner, whose role is that of a **MANAGER,** keeping everyone in line and on track. The business owner's focus should most definitely be on **QUALITY and PROCESS**, because the moment they introduce others to their business in any way, they run the real risk of reducing quality. The business owner is not doing and controlling everything within the business as in the previous stage. Focusing on process while working through this stage is vital. Most small business owners are fearful of introducing others into their business simply because they can't control what they do. It is absolutely correct that you can't control what another person does. Trying to do so will drive you crazy. Once business owners realise they can't control people but they can control process, then this very real fear is reduced. Cashflow at this stage is **ASSISTED**. It's not wholly and solely the business owners producing it.

Butterfly

The butterfly stage, the beautiful butterfly, is all about freedom. The BM model indicates this business model to be **INVESTMENT**. The business owner's role is that of a **LEADER.** There's a big difference between a manager and a leader, in fact I have a whole workshop series based around that. (Check out Authentic Leadership on my website if you're interested.) In this stage, the business owner's focus is on **VISION**, providing the insights and direction of the business journey for them, their team, and all their stakeholders. Cashflow may enter the realm of **PASSIVE,** where income is generated whether the owner attends work or not, perhaps even when they're sleeping.

Pretty simple, huh? As I mentioned earlier, one more thing to note about the BM model is that there is no right or wrong and the stages are not always linear, particularly when a business is in a growth or transition phase. Your client may identify their business as being mostly in the caterpillar stage, but may be focusing on quality and process in preparation for bringing in team members. Or they may identify their business as mostly in the chrysalis stage, but may be moving their role from manager to leader and their focus to vision, with increased business strategic advice and personal and professional development in preparation for taking the business to the next level.

I'd like to say one more thing about the BM model. It may look simplistic but when used to its best advantage with clients it packs a powerful punch. I've found myself plenty of times throughout my career, as I'm sure you have too, trying to explain to a client why their business is not delivering the results they want, and the financial reality of their business decisions. Many times, I avoided having this discussion for fear of the client's reaction.

By consistently working with clients using the BM model as your foundation, your clients may need just a little prod from you but they'll start to work out the answers for themselves. I've seen it happen time and time again.

A coach stimulates the client's self-discovery by asking powerful questions.

A coach is not an 'expert' but a facilitator of learning.

A coach helps people move from where they are now to where they want to be.

Using the BM model, clients will start to plot their own way forward, seeking your advice and assistance as their chosen advisor. The BM model supports and guides both you as the advisor and your client on the business advice journey.

Now that you know more about the BM model, I want to share with you my number one tip to successfully roll it out to your clients.

Just show them. Introduce them to the BM model using the Client Introduction Script you can download from my website: https://lyndasteffens.com/bonuses Have them complete the interactive version of the BM model while you chat, and then use that to start asking them questions about their business in the context of Business Metamorphosis®.

Your clients will be enthralled, because no-one they trust as much as you has ever bothered to look at or ask about their business and offer them help to move forward.

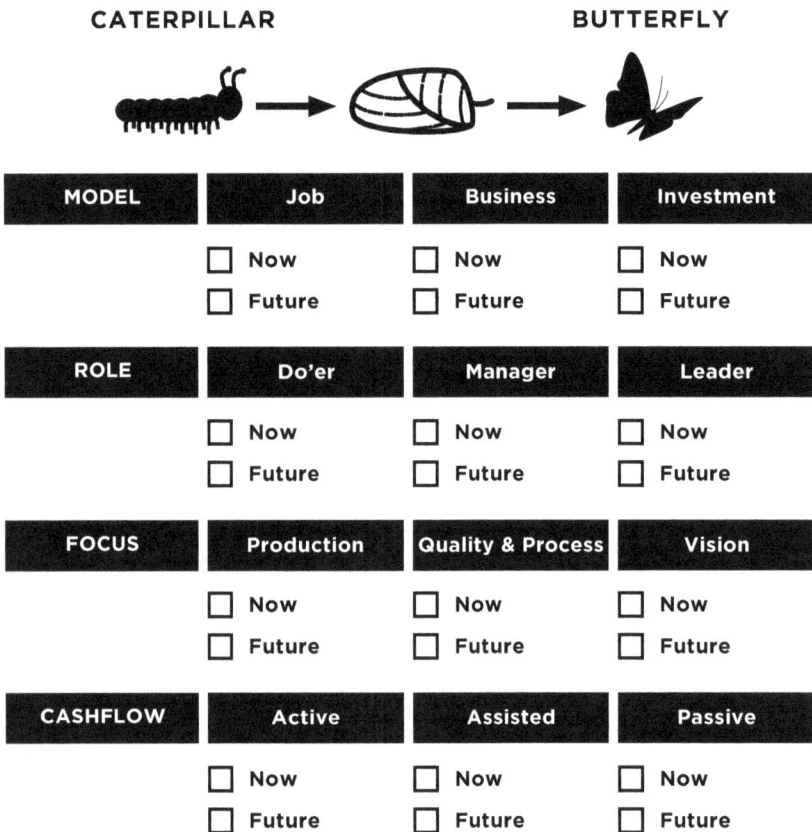

CATERPILLAR　　　　　　　　**BUTTERFLY**

MODEL	Job	Business	Investment
	☐ Now	☐ Now	☐ Now
	☐ Future	☐ Future	☐ Future

ROLE	Do'er	Manager	Leader
	☐ Now	☐ Now	☐ Now
	☐ Future	☐ Future	☐ Future

FOCUS	Production	Quality & Process	Vision
	☐ Now	☐ Now	☐ Now
	☐ Future	☐ Future	☐ Future

CASHFLOW	Active	Assisted	Passive
	☐ Now	☐ Now	☐ Now
	☐ Future	☐ Future	☐ Future

Figure 2.2 The Business Metamorphosis® Interactive Model

Just Start

As accountants, we naturally analyse everything and then analyse it again to be sure. There's no 80/20 for us, it's 100% or nothing.

Challenge yourself and just start. It won't be perfect but you'll have started.

Wearing Two Hats

Imagine yourself with two hats. The first one is the compliance expert hat and the second one is the business advisor/coach hat. In your mind's eye, you might associate a different colour with each of the hats, or have a feather in one. I love attending horseracing events, so my coach hat is a beautiful, elaborate concoction of colour, flowers, and feathers. If you're going to wear a hat you may as well stand out, I say.

Let's say you've just had a compliance meeting with clients where they've signed their tax returns. Now, you'd like to introduce them to Business Metamorphosis®. By way of segue, say, 'I'm going to take my compliance expert hat off for a few minutes and put my business advisor hat on. Is that okay?' Don't worry; they will never say no it's not okay. Visualise taking one hat off and replacing it with the other as you're saying it. This will help you not only transition the conversation but remind and focus yourself that you're switching to advisor mode. This will help you use The Coach Approach.

Let me tell you the story about when I first realised the power and potential of combining accounting and coaching, and why it's so important to change your conversations and engage with clients differently to do your job properly.

As I've mentioned, I went from practising accounting to being a practice manager and then into consulting, speaking, and coaching. Before I began focusing exclusively on accountants, I delivered business coaching. I was coaching Nathan, a client who wanted my help with growing his business. He was a big picture thinker and needed someone like me, someone who understood the importance of information and detail and instinctively used systems and processes, to help him take his sole trader business to the next level. We were discussing a new service he wanted to introduce, and I was explaining the importance of pricing and of knowing the numbers, specifically the new service's breakeven point.

I knew how to work this out but I was his coach, not his accountant, and I didn't want to step on his accountant's toes. So one of Nathan's action items for the month was to phone his accountant and ask what it would entail to do a simple costing exercise for his new service.

What I failed to do was ask Nathan what his relationship with his accountant was like and whether he felt comfortable asking this question. Guess what? Nathan came back the next month without having spoken to his accountant. When we talked about it, he gave several reasons.

He had identified his accountant with just doing his tax returns. His accountant had never asked about his business before, so why would they be interested in doing a pricing exercise now?

Nathan felt the cost of his tax returns was high and so his expectation of the price for this exercise was too high to consider even asking. If he didn't value the tax returns, which he saw as the accountant's speciality, how on earth would he get value for a pricing exercise, was his reasoning.

He was a little afraid to ask his accountant for help for fear of feeling inadequate and silly. The accountant had always conducted themselves in a courteous, professional, but expert manner and in Nathan's mind, this was not conducive to asking for help.

How many of your clients do you think feel this way about you? Many clients say they don't phone their accountant for help because it will cost them too much.

Just because we have been trusted experts does not mean we have fostered open-ended client relationships where clients are comfortable asking for assistance and advice.

When I was developing the BM model, I showed it to my partner who had just started his own small business. He had not been in business before and had no experience running a business. He just knew that he no longer wanted to work for someone else and so starting his own business was the answer.

On the other hand, I had the great privilege of being born into a small business family. My immediate family, my extended family, and friends' families all had businesses. Business runs through my veins and I quite obviously continued to expand my business knowledge by becoming an accountant. I've spent my whole life around business, instinctively understanding how business impacts not only the business owner but their families and their communities at large. What I took for granted was that everyone understood this. Silly, silly, me. How on earth can anyone understand this unless they've experienced it and even then, going into business is always a steep learning curve regardless of life experience, education, or background.

When I explained the BM model to my partner, he immediately understood it. I could see the light bulb moments happening for him right before my eyes. Straightaway, he plotted the stage he was at and saw the gap between his 'now' and 'the future' he wanted. That was when I knew I was onto something.

When people go into business, whether it's for the first time or not, they often wonder what the future looks like, what their journey will hold, how are they going to tackle problems as they arise. They look to accountants to help them and give them advice.

But with our expert mindsets and our time-driven natures, we've hindered the advice relationship, shut off that resource in some respects because we've not cultivated an advisor relationship with our client. Let's not forget that for some business owners, the only person who might be remotely interested in hearing about their business and how it's going is you, their accountant. We should never underestimate that.

Using the BM Model: A Story

I was working with a husband and wife team who wanted to move their business from what I now identify as the caterpillar stage to the chrysalis stage. They had part-time employees and contractors working for them.

They had tried to transition a couple of times before, and had had awful trouble with employees. It cost their business a lot of money and the last time, they had lost the business altogether. They attributed their failure to having employees. I needed to show them that there were underlying issues that had resulted in the transition being unsuccessful, not the mere fact of employing people.

The key concept they had missed was their role in the transition. They had been focusing solely on business development and market growth, not on quality and process. The wheels soon fell off.

I explained the BM model to them by simply drawing it on an A3 sheet of paper. It wasn't the professional digital design I use today. Again, I saw the light bulb moments happen before my eyes. After that, I realised it wasn't a coincidence. This thing made sense, it really worked. I was buoyed to develop it further.

But it wasn't quite as easy as that. Even though my clients saw that they needed to focus on quality and process while transitioning to the next stage, they found it challenging and felt it was counterproductive. When they started working on quality and process, they were simply not getting as much work done. For the first time, they were working **on** their business and not **in** it.

I continued to encourage and support them through the process of taking the time to develop processes around the tasks that were instinctive to them as business owners. They did these tasks every single day because they knew exactly what to do and the important things to focus on. I kept reminding them of their previous experiences, and how they didn't want to go down that path again. Over the next months, we continued to unpack their business and build the processes. They have successfully employed three staff members for more than two-and-a-half years now. Their business turnover and client base have grown substantially and their work–life balance has improved immensely.

Once you introduce your clients to the BM model, they will want more. Don't worry about or fear the next steps. I've got that all covered for you. Remember, Business Metamorphosis® is made up of two parts. In this chapter, we've focused on the model. The process comes next. You'll introduce your clients to the model, and then back it up with the process. Soon, you'll be successfully navigating Business Metamorphosis® and consistently delivering high-powered business advisory solutions to your clients – who will love you for it.

Remember ...

Just Start

As accountants, we naturally analyse everything and then analyse it again to be sure. There's no 80/20 for us, it's 100% or nothing.

Challenge yourself and just start. It won't be perfect but you'll have started.

Out of Your Comfort Zone

Yes, this is new, yes, this is different, yes, it will be foreign to you and yes, it will take practice and effort.

Concerns?

As you've been reading this chapter, you might have some concerns about introducing the BM model to your clients. There might be some red flags for you, such as, 'It's so simple that it's ridiculous, I can't possibly use that.'

Yes, the BM model is simple. That's the sheer beauty of it and why your clients will instantly connect to it. In the context of business advice, you need to break down your expert mindset that you use for compliance, and stop overcomplicating things with tax law and accounting principles. Your clients just want simple and easy.

The expert mindset reinforces that your value lies in complex, detailed information and having all the answers. For business advisory, it is dead wrong.

You might also think that clients come to you for accounting advice, not advisory services. Remember Nathan's story: do not underestimate the power of building open and honest client relationships based on an advisor/coach mindset. More to the point, always conducting yourself as an expert with clients can damage the relationship.

Just show some of your business clients the BM model and watch their reaction. They'll instinctively want to talk more about it because it's simple, it's easy, and it's something they understand, instead of feeling silly and inadequate in front of an expert.

You might also think that your clients are more sophisticated than what this model could possibly offer them. Every client in every business is on a journey, and every business has a life cycle. All business owners want to understand their journey and what's in front of them. Very few small businesses are at the stage that you could call them a complete and true butterfly. Even if they are, remaining a butterfly is hard work and they will need your ongoing support and guidance. To my mind, there is not one small business in the world that you couldn't help by introducing them to Business Metamorphosis®.

Actions to Take After Reading This Chapter

1. Download the Business Metamorphosis® interactive PDF and plot your own business.

2. Download the Business Metamorphosis® Client Introduction Script.

3. Introduce your client to Business Metamorphosis® at your next meeting.

Additional Information/Resources

- Business Metamorphosis® Client Introduction Script

- Business Metamorphosis® model PDF

- Business Metamorphosis® model interactive PDF

You will find the links to download all the documents listed under the above two headings here: https://lyndasteffens.com/bonuses

Ready for the first 'D' DISCOVER? Let's get cracking.

3

Time to DISCOVER

The smart ones ask when they don't know. And, sometimes, when they do

— Malcolm Forbes[6]

---

6 Amazon.com, 2019

DISCOVER is the first and most important of the three Ds. It's a free meeting of 30 to 45 minutes and it can be done over the phone. DISCOVER is the first step to understanding what your client wants from their business.

A successful DISCOVER meeting will have clients signing advisory proposals on the spot, no questions asked.

In this chapter, I share the six steps to running a successful DISCOVER meeting. It's powerful, it's easy, and all you need to do is follow a script.

People need reasons before they want answers. As accountants, we've been conditioned to jump straight into giving answers. We're not so good at providing reasons.

DISCOVER will give your client a reason to work with you. Follow the process step by step, and your client will have a compelling reason to work with you every single time. And all you did was ask.

Change a client's state from pain to pleasure by investigating where their business is now and where they want it to be in the future. Awaken their passion and belief that they can have that future with your guidance and support, your vital role in their business journey.

Deliver a state of clarity to your clients that they will have never experienced before. The DISCOVER process unequivocally shows them that they do not want to remain where their business is now. They wouldn't be talking to you otherwise. Together, explore your client's business 'now' and business 'future' and ignite their compulsion to move towards the future with you as the solution and their trusted advisor.

A recent survey of accounting firms showed that only half earn more than 10% of their total turnover from diversified services or advisory offerings. Nine out of 10 expect the demand for these advisory services to increase over the next two years.

My question is, how are you going to convert the increase in demand for advisory services, or will you simply miss out?

Wonder what your client really wants? Ask. Don't tell

— *Lisa Stone*[7]

If as an industry we fail to transition from a functional role to a vital one, and fail to convert the increasing demand for advisory services, our clients will undeniably find what they want elsewhere, thus forcing on traditional accounting businesses a continuing reliance on compliance and price competition.

Looking to the future, if accountants are not seen as viably offering these vital services to businesses, then with technological advances and artificial intelligence, how long do you think it will be before alternative service providers find a way to deliver the compliance services that accountants currently offer? I guarantee it won't be long.

Let's start with three of my top tips.

Tip 1: DISCOVER Is All About Questions, Not Answers

Purely by asking questions, you will create a powerful reason for your client to work with you. And there are a lot of questions. Get prepared: download the Meeting Script, Notes Template, and 10 Bonus Questions here: https.//lyndasteffens.com/bonuses

Below, we'll quickly chat about the first two questions, as you'll use these over and over again.

---

7   A-Z Quotes, 2019

Question 1: 'What Else?'

This question is a little beauty. When I'm coaching and consulting, it's my go-to question. Why? Because when used with the power of silence, it works every single time. You may find the meeting stalls from time to time because clients are not used to talking to you as an advisor, or they are not quite sure how to answer a question. When that happens, you just need to ask, 'What else?' You can ask this as often as you like, however many times it takes to elicit an answer.

People are very good at deflecting focus away from themselves. Sometimes, clients don't want to speak about things that might be hard to admit or face up to. Asking 'what else' gives clients that gentle nudge so you get all the answers you need.

Question 2: 'If You Did Know, What Would It Be?'

This one is a cracker, a real trickster. You might be thinking, I can't ask a client that. Well, I'm telling you, you absolutely can and you will. When you understand the true power of this process and that it will 100% benefit your client, you'll have no trouble asking this question. Remember: clients aren't used to talking to you in this way, they're only used to listening to you. You've not asked them any questions before, certainly none like this, so during DISCOVER they are likely to say several times in response to your questions, 'I don't know' or 'I'm not sure'. This question does the trick by giving them a little poke to keep them moving forward.

My own business coach Sharon uses these two questions on me all the time. Even though I know they're coming, and I know exactly what she's doing, I also know she's trying to help me get to the bottom of an issue or situation for myself. It's my answer that's important, not hers. Hers doesn't count. She's not in any way being pushy (although she's not shy about giving me a size seven in the rear end when I need one), and neither will you be.

I'm the type of person whose mind goes blank the moment you ask me something or tell me to speak. This happens to a lot of introverts because we process thoughts internally, not externally. You're probably like this and some of your clients might be too. Often, when I'm asked a question, my natural response is 'I don't know'. Sharon simply looks at me and asks, 'If you did know, what would it be?' You know what? Given a little bit of time and prompting, I do know.

Tip 2: There Is Only One Solution

There are no accounting and tax questions or answers in DISCOVER. If you start fielding questions from your client and providing answers, you won't get the result. There is only one solution available to you to give a client in the DISCOVER process, and that is to move to the next step, the second 'D' – DIG. We'll explore that further in the next chapter.

Facilitating, not Participating

You're asking questions, not providing answers.

You won't know the answers.

Tip 3: Reasons Are Emotional

Question 3: 'How Does That Make You Feel?'

DISCOVER is about creating a reason to work with you. Just like wants, reasons are emotionally based. Hence, the third question, 'How does that make you feel?'

Think about your business, or the business of a family member or friend. Is it non-emotional for them? Absolutely not! Aside from their home, a business will be the most emotionally invested and emotionally charged asset a person may ever own.

DISCOVER is about connecting with your clients on an advisor level, person to person, not on an expert level where you just tell them what to do. Remember: you are only asking questions, not investigating their feelings, or expanding on their feelings. These are personal to your client. Neither are you solving any emotional problems. You're only asking how something makes your client feel.

Your Value

Your value to all those around you is not in answers. It is clearly and undeniably in questions.

I know we're accountants, we talk numbers, we refer to reports and financial statements. We can't possibly ask about feelings ... can we? Yes, we can, and it's important that we do.

A coach stimulates a client's self-discovery by asking powerful questions.

People buy from those they know, like, and trust. You've got the trust. You need the know and the like. This will help you do that, so be comfortable and confident in asking about feelings.

Six-Step DISCOVER Meeting

Okay, let's move onto the six steps of running a successful DISCOVER meeting. If you have already downloaded the DISCOVER Meeting Script, then grab it so it's handy. If you haven't, then please do so as you'll need it to follow through on the next part of this chapter. I'm not going to elaborate on the whole script word for word. It's there for you to use and practise with. What I will be doing is breaking down the six steps and highlighting the important points to help you run a successful DISCOVER meeting.

DISCOVER meetings are usually best done over the phone, because clients can get distracted when they see you taking notes. They might think, 'That must be bad/good, they're writing it down.'

The most vital thing is to FOLLOW THE SCRIPT! If you don't, the meeting will not work and you won't get the result you need. You won't have created a strong enough reason for your client to work with you.

Before the Meeting

Set up your DISCOVER Meeting Template. If you're doing the meeting over the phone, the best option for notetaking is a whiteboard. Not only do you get to stand up and move around, which helps the meeting flow, but you have heaps of space to write your notes. Then you simply take a photo of the whiteboard when you're finished, send it to your admin team (if you have one), and save it to the client file for later reference. Encourage your client to take photos of the notes on their phone so they can refer back to them later. If you're doing a Zoom or Skype meeting, you can use a notepad. For a face-to-face meeting, you could use either a notepad or a whiteboard.

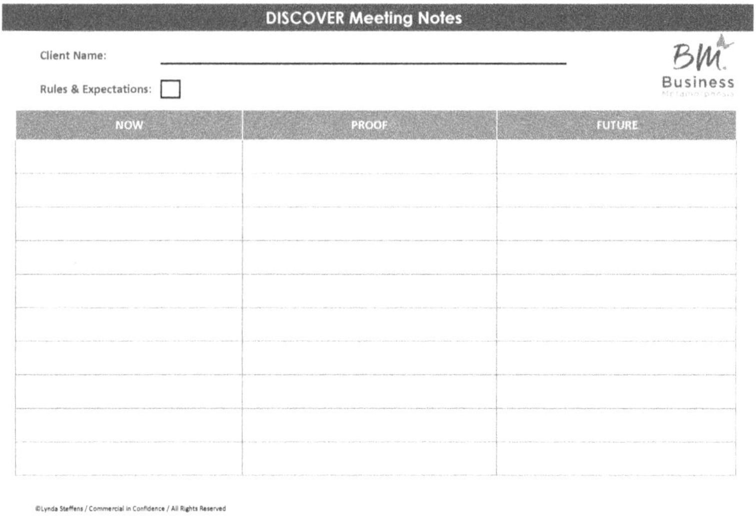
DISCOVER Meeting Notes

Client Name: ______________________

Rules & Expectations: ☐

NOW	PROOF	FUTURE

©Lynda Steffens / Commercial in Confidence / All Rights Reserved

Figure 3.1 DISCOVER Meeting Template

Write your client's name in the top left of your DISCOVER Meeting Template, every single time. Don't underestimate this seemingly simple action and what appears to be a small and unimportant piece of information. Not that you're going to forget who you're talking to, but introverts' minds can sometimes go blank. Because you're processing a lot of information at any one time, names can be the first thing that get thrown out. Having your client's name right there in front of you will not only stop you from going blank but will also prompt you to use it regularly throughout the meeting, creating that personal connection.

Check your calendar to find a couple of days where you could complete the next stage of Business Metamorphosis® with your client. These timeslots should be within seven to 21 days. Try not to leave completing the next stage for longer than that. Keep these timeslots handy as you'll need them at the end of the meeting.

Use your Tools

Make sure you have a copy of the Business Metamorphosis® model, the DISCOVER Script, and the 10 Bonus Questions on hand at all times. They will keep you focused, make you feel safe and secure, and give you the structure you need for the powerful client conversations that deliver consistent and meaningful messages.

Step 1: Rules and Expectations

It's crucial before you start any DISCOVER meeting to set the rules and expectations for it. Remember: clients aren't used to having meetings like this with you. They need to understand what's going to happen.

Tell them:

- That the meeting is likely to take 30 to 45 minutes, but it may take longer so it's a good idea if they don't have to rush off to another meeting straightaway.

- You won't be talking about accounting and tax today, in fact, you won't even mention it. Set the expectation that the meeting is simply about connecting with them as a business owner and a person. You want to understand where their business is now and where you want it to be in the future. You will get to all the 'how-tos' at a later stage. This meeting is the start.

- You might like to use the wearing of two hats analogy to help clients visualise the difference between accountant and coach. Say to your client, 'I'm going to take off my accountant hat and put on my advisor/coach hat. Is that okay?' This will help you switch into The Coach Approach.

- Switch straight over into the DISCOVER script, tell them they need to play 'full out', that is, they need to be totally honest and upfront with you. The reason is so you can deliver the most value possible in the shortest time, just like it says in the script. Some clients might say, 'Oh, I'm a bit scared now.' Just reassure them that they will be fine and they'll have all the answers when they need them. They are the expert in their business, not you.

Step 2: Now

The first step was quick and easy. On to Step two.

In this step, you are finding out about your client's current business, family life, relationships, health, and so on.

Clients use your accountancy practice for their financial affairs, so you're going to focus most of your energy on your client's business situation. However, a great coach (and a good accountant for that matter) knows that you cannot separate business from personal. We're human beings and it doesn't work like that. You need the full picture. How many times in your professional career have you seen businesses affect relationships for the worst, or relationships affect a business? Events such as a marriage breakdown, or the health of the business owner or one of their family members, can completely change the course of a business, regardless of the business plan.

Start by confirming some basic information that you and your client already know, just to get things moving: the type of business, last year's turnover, the number of employees. For example, 'Okay, you have a mechanics workshop, and last year you turned over around $450,000 with two employees.' That's it, don't go into any more detail, just stick to a couple of basics.

Next ask, 'Tell me what's going on with your business?' In almost all situations, this simple question unleashes a lot of information. Remember: take notes using the DISCOVER Meeting Template. Your client might take a little while to warm up. Remember Question 1: 'What else, what else, what else?'

Facilitating not Participating

You're asking questions, not providing answers.

You won't know the answers.

As you're working through DISCOVER, hearing about your client's business, you may be tempted to interrupt and provide them with answers and solutions. DON'T. Remember Tip 2, there is only one solution, and stick to the DISCOVER script. You won't be able to stop solutions from popping into your mind. It's how accountants are built and why we're so good at what we do, but DISCOVER is not the time or place for them. You could note down your solution as a way of getting it out of your mind, but avoid discussing it with your client. If you do, you will not get the result you want. Follow the DISCOVER script and the process will work.

Step 3: Proof

This step is where you will first start to introduce some negative energy to the meeting. I find it the most challenging step but after doing it so many times, I realise it's an essential element. It's where the power of the DISCOVER meeting lies. What is also challenging about this step is that accountants are nice people, and it's not nice to have your clients reflect on negative things, nor easy to discuss these hard things with them.

Out of Your Comfort Zone

Yes, this is new, yes, this is different, yes, it is foreign to you, and yes, it will take practice and effort.

Start Proof by asking your client to rate their business out of 10. The DISCOVER Script shows you exactly what to say and once they give you the answer, how to proceed from there.

Now is the time to prod, poke, nudge, and keep digging, using the questions in the DISCOVER Script and the 10 Bonus DISCOVER Questions. You want to achieve a list of as many 'bad' feeling words about how staying at x of out 10 makes them feel. This is crucial to the DISCOVER process. You'll use these words in future meetings to help keep your client focused on what's at stake. Don't worry; you'll get a list of 'good' words too, a bit later on. Don't be afraid to repeat yourself and alternate the questions over and over. Just when you think you've got everything from your client, ask a couple more questions.

Reminding clients of the rules and expectations in this step is very helpful. Acknowledge that some of these questions might be a little hard to answer, but that they said they would be open and honest with you and play full out.

You Don't Need the Story

To avoid talking about negative stuff, your client at this stage is likely to try and elaborate, to give you the story behind why they feel a certain way. You don't need the story. You have that already from Step 2 Now. You need to be forthright here and move them on. Just say, 'Yep, I've got it, what else?' This will give them a gentle nudge.

Reassurance goes a long way. Reassure your client that they're doing great, that you'll only stay in this negative spot a little longer, and that it's a really important part of the process.

It's essential to bring your client down into a negative state because it allows you to bring them back up into a positive state. The lower the negative state, the greater the gap to bring them up to the positive, which makes the reason to work with you much more significant.

The DISCOVER Script gives you five questions. You need to repeat these, perhaps changing them up a little so you don't sound like a robot. Throw in some of the Bonus Questions. Delve into what it means to your client to stay at x out of 10 before completing your list of 'bad' words. Simply asking the five questions once over is not enough.

Repetition = Significance

Mark with an asterisk (*) anything your client repeats. If they repeat it a third time, mark it with a second asterisk (**). Clearly, anything repeated is significant and you'll want to rummage around in these weighty issues as you move through your DISCOVER meeting.

The next step in Proof is to elicit a universal measurement of what the personal cost to your client would be if their business remained at x out of 10. Several of the Bonus Questions help you with this. The answer you are looking for is not a logical monetary one, as feelings and personal cost cannot be quantified in this way. You're looking for answers like 'priceless', 'billions', 'beyond the universe', 'more than life', 'immeasurable', 'infinity' ... Remember: this is about feelings, not logical numbers.

To help your client with this you might like to repeat some of the bad feeling words they have already used, particularly if they have an asterisk (*) beside them. Prompt your client by saying, 'If your business remained at x out of 10, and it never got any better or maybe it even got a little worse, how would you measure the personal cost to you and your family?'

The questions in the DISCOVER Script and the 10 Bonus Questions are some of the most compelling you will ever ask a client – without a single reference to accounting or tax.

 A coach stimulates the client's self-discovery by asking powerful questions.

I have a very good friend who says, 'An honest no is better than a false yes.' With Proof, you will come to understand that it's critical to talk with clients about what is sometimes hard and uncomfortable stuff. At most, this negative space will last no longer than 10 or 15 minutes. Also, you're doing this for your client, to connect them with their why. It's not to make you feel comfortable, so push through.

Proof is the trickiest part of DISCOVER to master, mainly because it's so very different from what you're used to. But don't worry. If you don't get it right every time, you'll generally find that your clients already have a lot of trust in you as their accountant and that by just going through the process, you'll get the desired result.

The final step in Proof is to reassure your client that they've done really well and thank them for playing full out with you because it was really important.

Now you're going to talk about some positive things.

Step 4: Future

Okay, now we're into the good stuff, the future. You've looked at what your client's business is now and how they rate it out of 10. Now, you get to explore what their business as a 10 out of 10 will look like.

The DISCOVER Script provides all the questions you need and the prompts to help your client focus on their business future. Ask them in different ways and don't be afraid of repeating yourself. Once you have all the detail, then move onto how this would make them feel.

Your goal here is to get a long list of 'good' words about how having a 10 out of 10 business makes them feel. You'll use your list of good words in future meetings to reinforce to your client why they need to continue to work on their business with your support. The scripts relating to the later chapters show you how to cement the gap in your client's mind every time you meet with them, by combining a couple of the good and bad words at the start of each and every meeting.

Take Notes

Sometimes, you may get so wrapped up in what your client is saying that you'll forget to take notes. You can always make these after a meeting, but it's easier if you write them down throughout the meeting.

Keep going with getting 'good' feeling words until your notes page is full. Then it's time to move to the universal measurement. Gathering the universal measurement is the same process as the third step. It just has a positive connation rather than a negative one.

Use the Bonus Question, 'If you got all of this, what would it be worth to you?'

As in Step 3, the answer you are looking for is not a logical monetary one because feelings and personal value cannot be quantified in this way. You're looking for the same answers: 'priceless', 'billions', 'beyond the universe', 'more than life', 'immeasurable', 'infinity'. You're talking about feelings, not logical numbers.

To help your client with this you might like to repeat some of the good feeling words they have already used, particularly if these have an asterisk (*) beside them.

With universal measurements, your client will be of the mindset that they are willing to do almost anything to get them the future they want, which moves them perfectly into the next step, Desire.

Step 5: Desire

Your goal in this step is for your client to rate their commitment to achieving the future they have just imagined as 10 out of 10. If you've followed the DISCOVER Script, you'll find that most people will go straight to 10 out of 10, because you've elicited the universal measurements for both Proof and Future appropriately.

For clients who don't go straight to a 10 out of 10, there are a couple of Bonus Questions to help them get there. It is also worth repeating that they are not rating themselves on knowing what to do or how to do it. That comes later. Once you've questioned them a little further, repeat the question, 'What would you rate your commitment and desire to get your business to a 10/10?'

Some clients need a little extra encouragement. There are always those who think, 'I'm not perfect, no-one's a 10 out of 10, I wouldn't sell my soul,' etc. That's exactly what I said to my coach when she did this with me. I said I was a 9 out of 10. She quickly and expertly let me know that no-one would be asking me to sell my soul. She said, 'Let's completely remove any concern you have about selling your soul. Now, what do you rate yourself out of 10?' I said, 'Okay, taking that out, I'm definitely a 10 out of 10.' You see, if she hadn't probed, she would not have known how to handle my objection and get me to a 10 out of 10.

It's a huge confidence builder to take your client from what appears to be their lowest of low in Proof, and help them paint the future they desire for themselves and their family. Their 10 out of 10 is absolutely possible.

Now you're ready for the final step. Even if you don't have a 10 out of 10 answer, you move to the final step regardless.

Step 6: Next Steps

In this final step, you provide the one and only solution you need to deliver in DISCOVER: proceed to the next D, DIG.

You might say something like, 'Great, I'd love to work with you at a 10 out of 10. Your next step is to do a DIG session. In DIG, we extend far beyond what we have today. We completely unpack your business and unearth what keeps you up at night. We do this so we can know exactly how to move forward and help you deliver your 10 out of 10. You'll have even more clarity than you gained today about your business and how to move forward. DIG takes around two to three hours of us working together to get everything out on the table. It costs $xxxx. I've checked my calendar and I could do this with you next week on x if that suits you?'

DIG is the only solution you offer at this time. Offering client advisory services now is too early. Your client is not ready for them yet, even if they're asking for them, and frankly, neither are you. You've not delved deep enough into your client's business to truly know what they want. You might think you know (and more often than not you'd be right), but until you turn their need into a want, you won't successfully engage your client with advisory services. We'll investigate this concept further in the next chapter.

This is why it's so important to have checked your calendar and have a couple of timeslots available in the next week or two to complete the DIG. Clients won't want to wait.

Yay! You've done it, made it to the end of the six steps. Easy, right? As I said at the beginning, this was one of the big implementation chapters so you might feel like going back and reading parts of it again. That's to be expected. It's pretty big.

Summary Tips

A couple of tips to wrap up ...

Don't be afraid of the power of silence. You may find from time to time that DISCOVER meetings can stall. Even when you ask, 'What else?' your client might still be coming up with blanks. Just remain silent and let them think about it. Something will come to them.

He or she who speaks first loses, right! So, get comfortable with using a bit of silence, it's extremely powerful.

A coach is not an 'expert' but a facilitator of learning.

Out of Your Comfort Zone

Yes, this is new, yes, this is different, yes, it is foreign to you, and yes, it will take practice and effort.

Let me tell you a quick story about an early DISCOVER meeting I had with one of my accounting clients. The first meeting with him went very well. We talked briefly about our businesses and how we might work together. I introduced him to Business Metamorphosis®. He agreed to do a DISCOVER meeting with me and we booked it in.

Matthew is a very positive fellow. Nothing gets him down. If something happens, he just shifts the goalposts and keeps moving forward. It seems that nothing gets in his way.

When it came to Step 3, Proof, I found it quite difficult as there was no way he was going down into the negative. He kept shifting the goalposts and moving forward, and I kept asking him questions every which way I could think of, but he was so positive that he was able to turn any negative into a positive and had no negative feelings. He kept saying that wouldn't happen.

Are you having a light bulb moment yet about what you would have done? I hope you're thinking exactly what I should have done: remind him of the rules and expectations. He had agreed to play full out with me, to tell me how he would feel if these negative situations were to occur. I didn't ask him that.

We got all the way through the Proof meeting and he told me he was 10 out of 10 committed to do whatever he needed to do. However, when I told him what the next steps were, he was not willing to proceed. This was simply because I hadn't been able to bring him low enough in the Proof step.

Now, it's a given that you will win some and lose some but if you practise, it will greatly increase your success with DISCOVER meetings.

Practise

Practise, practise, practise.

Don't fool yourself into thinking you can do this without practice, even though I know you'll probably try more than once. As accountants, we're extremely time conscious so we think, hang it, I'll wing it. I guarantee you won't get a great result if you take this approach. How do I know? Because I did this too! Role-play with a team member or a friend. Put in the time and you'll get a great result.

Speaking Aloud

Make sure you speak aloud when you practise. Don't just think about what you would say by running through it in your mind. While internal monologue is the accountant's go-to technique (we love to do things in our heads), it won't work for practising what to say. As an introvert, you'll struggle to produce the words when you need them if all you've done is think them through. The cat, the dog, or even the chair works well to practise on.

This chapter has a great deal of information to get through. After reading it, I wager that you're thinking you can't do it, that it's not for you.

You're probably thinking you wouldn't even know where to start, or how to suggest a meeting like this to a client.

Well, that's an easy one. You won't need to suggest it to your clients. The moment you show them Business Metamorphosis®, they're going to want to talk about their business more. Once you've introduced them to Business Metamorphosis® and taken 10 to 15 minutes to explain the BM model, they will want to know what to do next.

Here's your opening to say, 'Let's have a DISCOVER meeting to investigate this further.' Book the meeting with them. Tell them a little about the DISCOVER meeting: how long it will take, that you will be exploring where their business is now, where they would like to see it in the future, and most importantly, how they feel about their business future. Nothing further.

You might also be thinking that you're very likely to go into solution mode in the DISCOVER meeting. The clients will ask you an accounting or tax question and you'll get bogged down talking about accounting and tax.

No, you won't. Not if you follow the DISCOVER Script, and I can't reiterate enough how important it is to **practise** by speaking aloud. There is no accounting and tax in DISCOVER for a reason. You don't need it and after a few tries, you won't feel the need to mention it at all.

Remember: you set the rules and expectations at the start of the meeting. No accounting and tax. You're not even going to mention it. Repeat this if you need to. Honestly, following the DISCOVER Script makes this easy and you will be okay.

Perhaps you've tried something like this before and it didn't work. The client took control of the meeting and you didn't end up engaging them in advisory services in the end.

My only response is that it wouldn't have been Business Metamorphosis® and the 3Ds. You would not have been conducting a DISCOVER meeting with a DISCOVER Script like this. Follow the DISCOVER Script, follow the system, and practise the process. It will work. I have no doubt.

Need More Help? Book a Workshop

Nonetheless, if you still feel you need a little more help with DISCOVER, check out when our next Business Metamorphosis® workshop is. It won't be far away. In this three-day workshop, we spend half a day extensively on running a DISCOVER meeting because we recognise it's a big step and very different from what we're used to doing as accountants.

Once you've done the workshop, there are some implementation plans on offer to attendees.

Don't forget to download the additional resources from the website https://lyndasteffens.com/bonuses and get cracking with actions at the end of the chapter.

Actions to Take After Reading This Chapter

1. Download the DISCOVER Script, Meeting Template and 10 Bonus Questions.

2. Role-play a DISCOVER meeting with one of your team, a friend, or a client who is also a friend. Read straight from the DISCOVER Script and have them answer the questions while you take notes.

3. Book a DISCOVER meeting with a client.

Additional Information/Resources

- DISCOVER Script

- DISCOVER Meeting Template

- 10 Bonus DISCOVER Questions

You will find the links to download all the documents listed under the above two headings here: https://lyndasteffens.com/bonuses

Rock 'n roll, let's get digging.

4

Time to DIG

Efficiency is doing things right; effectiveness is doing the right things

— *Peter Drucker*[8]

---

8   A-Z Quotes, 2019

DIG is the second of the 3Ds and the only D with a payment attached. Its sole purpose is to delve into your client's business and gather all the detail you need to understand exactly what your client wants to achieve from being in business. DIG encompasses 12 steps. These give you all the information you need to move to the third and final D, DELIVER.

DIG is designed to bridge the gap from paying annual compliance fees to making a regular monthly commitment for advisory services. It dramatically increases clients' take-up of these services.

You'll find it easier to follow through the chapter with the DIG Detailed Agenda in front of you. Go to https://lyndasteffens.com/bonuses and download it now.

But first, let's work through what you're trying to achieve when completing a DIG with your client.

Introducing clients to a regular financial commitment for advisory services doesn't need to be difficult. You may have already discovered, however, that trying this too early in a client engagement or relationship tends to have a high failure rate.

DIG accelerates the client relationship timeline. You'll successfully introduce clients to regular advisory services after just two meetings.

DIG increases your clients' confidence in you as an advisor and connects you with them as an advisory provider. It gives them astonishing clarity into where their business is now and what they want their business future to look like. Let your natural curiosity for all things business shine through and your clients will think you're the best thing since sliced bread, just because you are interested enough to ask.

In DIG, you can take full advantage of your information and analysis superpowers by:

- Skilfully helping clients unpack their business

- Unearthing what's important to them

- Drilling down into what keeps them up at night

- Expertly walking clients through their business journey and helping them identify the gaps in reaching their goal

- Strengthening and building rapport with your clients like never before, business owner to business advisor

- Finally bridging the gap between functional compliance services and vital advisory services as you help clients map out the next steps of their business journey.

Stop underestimating the value and trust that clients have in your advice and counsel. Remember: a client's accountant is often the only person they can talk openly and honestly to about their business. Take a deep dive into your client's business to show them that you're not only interested but that you understand their business and are invested in helping them on their business journey.

The No. 1 reason business owners leave accountants is that the accountant doesn't understand the client's business.

> *Prescription without diagnosis is malpractice*
> — *Dr Nancy Synderman*[9]

One of our weaknesses as accountants is to assume what clients want from us without ever bothering to ask them. By assessing our client's needs instead of asking them, we've held ourselves back from delivering our true potential as business advisors and doing the best job possible for them.

Failing to bridge the gap from functional to vital services, from expert to advisor, and not having clients regularly engage in advisory

---

9 Hoagland-Smith, 2019

services means that you will be forced to have an ongoing reliance on compliance to maintain your business. You'll be stuck doing work that doesn't excite you or your team. In my experience, this means business will just keep getting harder and harder. In fact, you might already be at the point where you just don't want to do it anymore. I see this more and more in the accounting industry. Don't let it happen to you. Engage with your clients and have them value what you do.

DIG is all about creating gaps.

You start by leveraging off the high-level strategic gaps you've so very skilfully created in the client's mind by having them interact with the Business Metamorphosis® model. You then move into the gaps you identified in DISCOVER, where you asked your client to rate their business out of 10. Their score obviously was not 10 out of 10. They have some way to go, which is why you're continuing to work with them. Your client identifies with the gaps and already sees you as the solution to bridging those gaps.

Always refer to you and your client as 'we'. You're a team. There is no 'U' or 'I' in team.

DIG does not necessarily widen the gap. It builds on the gaps, which you meticulously layer with detail, gaining clarity for both you and the client about what the gap is and how to bridge it.

Once again, DIG is all about asking questions. You want your client to realise they don't have the answers to a lot more questions about how they take their business from where they are now to where they want to be in the future. Just like DISCOVER, there are no answers in DIG, and there is only one solution. That's to move to the third D, DELIVER. If you've followed the process of introducing your client to Business Metamorphosis® and had a DISCOVER meeting, your client will already be looking for your help to bridge the gaps and answer the questions, but DIG is not the place to do that.

Facilitating not Participating

You're asking questions, not providing answers.

You won't know the answers.

Out of Your Comfort Zone

Yes, this is new, yes, this is different, yes, it is foreign to you, and yes, it will take practice and effort.

Okay, let's work through the DIG Detailed Agenda and the 12 steps. They're not 12 humungous steps, just 12 small steps that will have you running a successful DIG session right from the start. The 12 steps and tools introduced to you so far will ensure you have no trouble meeting with your client for two to three hours undertaking a DIG. But before you launch into it, there are some things you should do to prepare for the session.

The 12-Step DIG

This is just like the Boston Two Step – only longer, slightly more complicated, and without music. You could add music to your DIG session but I think you would find it distracting ... have you cottoned on that I like music and dancing? My apologies, I can't help it. I grew up in a rural region in South East Queensland and my family regularly attended country dances. I learned old-time dancing, a much older and less rigid form of ballroom dancing. It was loads of fun and I have many fond memories of that time ... I did warn you I would go off on a tangent from time to time.

Bring up a copy of the DIG Detailed Agenda so you can follow along with the 12-step process. Find this resource here: https://lyndasteffens.com/bonuses

Step 1 – Revisit the Gaps, Set Expectations, and Why We're Here

Every meeting in The Small Business Project starts with the why, including DIG.

Step 1 will take you five minutes at the most. Very simply, you revisit the gaps you have already created with your client. You also set expectations. The reason you're here is a natural by-product of doing those first two things.

At this point in your client's journey, you've created one major gap, the DISCOVER business rating score out of 10. The purpose of revisiting this score is to evoke all the emotions your client felt during their DISCOVER session, which can be quite emotional. Remind your client that you're here today to work together to build their business from x out of 10 to 10 out of 10. Remind them that being x out of 10 doesn't feel very good and if they were to stay that way, they said it would feel … Use a couple of the bad words you gathered in DISCOVER. Remember: business is emotional and it's crucial you use these emotional hooks to set every meeting off on the right foot.

Move onto setting expectations. Here, you explain that you'll help them piece together exactly where they are now in their business journey and where they would like to be in the future, showing them in detail what that looks like. They will gain clarity around where their business is at like never before, and you will be able to show them what their business journey will look like.

You'll be discussing core strategies for bridging the gaps between where they are now and where they want to be, and helping them prioritise those strategies as they move through their journey. At the end of the meeting, you'll finalise and give them their full Action Plan, which includes who's responsible for what and when those things need to be done. They will take the Action Plan with them and start working on it straightaway.

Step 2 – Business Metamorphosis® Overview

Step 2 is another small five-minute step at most, but fundamental to achieving the meeting outcomes. It continues the process of creating and revisiting gaps.

Use your Business Metamorphosis® model to step through the three key stages of caterpillar, chrysalis, and butterfly, and the four key elements of model, role, focus, and cashflow. If you need a reminder, revisit Chapter 2 Business Metamorphosis® for how to go about it. This may seem counterproductive to you, especially if the client has already seen and completed the BM interactive version, but it most definitely is not.

Time and time again, we make the mistake of not taking opportunities to talk about and demonstrate the value that we can deliver to clients as advisors. That value sits fairly and squarely in this simple little model and warrants a few minutes of time.

By revisiting the model and business lifecycle, you're reinforcing the gaps between your client's now and future, and laying down more groundwork to leverage from. Do not skip this step. Doing so will make the meeting much less effective and reduce your client's commitment to continuing the advisory journey with you. In truth, you should have the Business Metamorphosis® model with you at every single meeting from here on. I have no doubt you will use it in some form every single time.

Don't Set Yourself Up to Fail

Give yourself plenty of time, be prepared, gather information, follow the system, practise, and pick an easy target – that is, don't start with the most difficult client on your books.

Step 3 – Review or Complete Business Metamorphosis® Interactive Model

Take the next few minutes to either review your client's completed BM interactive model or have them complete it with you. Once you've explained the model, it's a simple matter for them to tick the now and future boxes they identify with. Some clients may wish to update the one they've done already by doing it again. You'll use this later in the meeting to help lead the discussion.

Step 4 – NOW Analysis

As accountants, we like data and concrete evidence so an easy place to start analysing a client's business is using their most recent financial results to see what's happening in their business right now.

I call this the NOW analysis.

Neither you nor your client can get this wrong.

Reassure your client that regardless of what this analysis shows, they should not feel self-conscious or nervous about revealing the information or how they feel about it. Tell them they're doing a great job by seeking help to move towards their future. You're there to help them and just like in DISCOVER, they need to be open and honest with you and play full out. That way, they'll get the best value from your time together.

I recommend gathering the following 10 pieces of data. I've included them in a grid for you as a bonus resource. Download the NOW and FUTURE Analysis Grid to help you set this out: https://lyndasteffens.com/bonuses Use the grid to set up your notes before the meeting.

1. Annual Turnover. Most recent completed financial year turnover in dollars.

2. Gross Profit. Most recent completed financial year gross profit in dollars and as a percentage (%).

3. Net Profit. Most recent completed financial year net profit in dollars and as a percentage (%).

4. Services & Products. A list of current services and products and the percentage (%) of sales each represents.

5. Clients or Customers. An estimate of client numbers and broadly speaking their types. The client/customer type will be dependent on your client's business. For example, residential vs commercial customers, or wholesale vs retail, or they may deal with two or three main industry types such as transport, mining, and primary producers. NB: Don't get caught up in the detail. A broad overview is all you need for the NOW analysis.

6. Staff Roles. The number of staff and their roles.

7. Owner(s) Age at their last birthday.

8. Owner(s) Salary, if they're paying themselves one.

9. Owner(s) Role and Duties. Current role and duties in the business.

10. Owner(s) Average Hrs Worked and Holidays. Looks to the owner(s) current work–life balance.

These 10 seemingly innocuous pieces of information paint a very clear picture of where your client's business is right now, and will no doubt evoke some great discussion. Remember: your client rarely has the opportunity to discuss this type of stuff with anyone. Because you're their accountant, someone they implicitly trust, they'll love it.

You'll find your client will be happy with some and not so happy with others, maybe even a little ill at ease. Reassure them again that they've done really well because now you have something to work with. They can't know if they're moving forward unless they know where they've been.

Your client may also want to discuss why they're happy or not so happy with the NOW. There's no need to shut them down but you do need to be conscious of time. The two to three hours will fly by before you know it. To help you move through the meeting agenda, tell your client that you'll be having a full discussion about what they like and don't like about their business in the SWOT analysis a little later on. There's no need to get bogged down in it now.

You will already have the first three pieces of information (1, 2, and 3 from the list above) from your client's financial statements. It's best that you help them calculate these anyway, explaining briefly as you go along why these numbers are important. You'll need to ask your clients to provide all other information.

I've allocated 15 minutes in the agenda for the NOW analysis but don't panic if it takes a bit longer. Some clients need to discuss particular items more than others do.

Step 5 – DISCOVER Business Rating

This is a really quick step, just a minute or two. Remind your client of the DISCOVER meeting. In Chapter 3 Time to DISCOVER, I said that you would continue to use three things from this meeting: the 'bad' words, the 'good' words, and the business rating out of 10. Reviewing this reinforces to your client why this process is crucial to their business journey and encourages a greater desire to continue it with you as their advisor.

All you need to do here is quickly say something like, 'Let's remember why we're here. It's to build a 10 out of 10 business for you. In DISCOVER, you told me you felt like your business was currently at x out of 10, that it made you feel ... (insert a couple of bad words), and that getting to a 10 out 10 would feel ... (insert two or three good words).' Write the business rating x/10 in the top left-hand corner of the whiteboard. Make sure you write it out of 10 (don't just put their score), then draw an arrow across to the top-right side and write '10/10'.

No-one wants to feel bad about their business; they want to feel good. What you have just done by this very simple exercise is reiterate it to them and put yourself in a position to help them feel good. Don't skip this step. It's one of the building blocks in the process. Leave it out and you may not get the result you want.

Gathering your Thoughts

If at any time you need to gather your thoughts, jot something down – on the whiteboard, the butchers paper, or sticky notes. It doesn't need to be anything of great importance. You can just say, 'I don't want to forget that so I'll just note it down now.' Meanwhile, you've had 30 seconds or so to gather your thoughts.

One of our challenges as introverts is speaking off the cuff. That's because we process thoughts internally, not externally like extroverts. Extroverts talk and think at the same time. We think then talk. I often say to clients, 'Give me a minute to think on that.' They generally think nothing of it. It's part of getting used to how I work.

Step 6 – Current Strategy and Vision

Step 6 is starting to get into the meatier stuff. Always keep in mind DIG is about creating gaps and questions in your client's mind. This is exactly what you will do by looking at their current strategy and vision. The gap here is about showing your client that they either have no strategy or vision in place, or they do but it doesn't make sense to them and they need to do something about it. Don't panic. This is not a strategic planning meeting. You don't need to know how to do it until later on, and I'll tell you all about how in Chapter 8 The Master Plan. Now, it's simply a review and assessment of their current strategies and visions – if they have any.

Quite a number of your small business clients may have no strategy or vision in place. It's very common. Do you have one for your business?

If a client does, it's likely to be something a marketing consultant wrote for their website, if they have a website that is. If they do, the best place to start is the vision and/or mission statements on their website. Have a quick discussion about the statements, what they mean to your client and if they relate to them in any way. Ninety-nine per cent of the time your client will have paid little attention to them and most likely say they were just something the marketing people did. True strategic foundation is something you hold to every single day. You can quote it in your sleep, your team can quote it in their sleep, it reflects why you are in business and how you go about conducting yourself in business, it drives all business decisions big and small, and it's the glue keeping your business on track. Businesses without a strategic foundation may grow, but long-term sustainable growth is founded on and maintained through strategy and vision.

If your client doesn't have a website or a strategy or a vision, no trouble. Once you explain to them the purpose of strategy and vision and why they need strong strategic foundations, you will have created the necessary gap. Note down on your Action Plan 'formulate strategic foundation'. That's what we'll walk through in Chapter 8 The Master Plan.

Exit plans are also within Step 6, as exiting is definitely a strategy. The questions to ask include: what is their exit plan, do they have one, have they even thought about it? The best time to put in place an exit strategy is when you start your business. The second-best time is now. Discuss with your client what their vision is for exiting the business. Will they sell it, or do they want to create a legacy for their children? Do they have children who will want to succeed them in the business? Do they want to build a butterfly business with passive income and hold onto that investment, passing it on through their estates?

There are many questions you can ask about exit plans in this step and it's okay if your client has not really thought about the answers. These can come later. When your client doesn't have all the answers, you will have created another gap for them. Add to your Action Plan, 'formulate exit plan'. Unfortunately, too many clients don't think about exiting until they're trying to do it, or something has forced them into doing it; perhaps health, finances, or economic influences. By then, it is way too late to realise the best outcomes for clients.

In the DIG session, you do not have time to formulate an exit plan. That's why you've written it on your Action Plan. Be warned: exit plans are right up your alley. You have the answers, but don't fall into the trap of telling your client what they need, not yet anyway.

Facilitating not Participating

You're asking questions, not providing answers.

You won't know the answers.

You need very little detail around strategy and vision or the exit plan. All you need to know is that your client has nothing concrete in place. Create the gap. Bridging the gap and helping your client to answer their questions comes in the form of Leading Edge Business™ in chapters 7 to 10. These outline exactly how to go about providing solutions. That's when you will focus on the money, numbers, tax, accounting, and financial areas of the business and draw on your collaborative network of professionals to help with anything you are unable to provide.

Step 7 – SWOT

Step 7 will wow your clients. Most small business owners have never had the chance to work thought a SWOT analysis before. As you know, they can be extremely eye-opening if the client is being completely open and honest and playing full out. It's a great time to remind your clients that while some of this might be a little confronting, it's best they put their whole effort behind it to get the greatest value.

I've allocated 30 minutes in the agenda for this step but it will depend on your client and where they're at.

Start by explaining what SWOT means because your client may not know: strengths, weaknesses, opportunities, and threats. And you guessed it: your objective is to create gaps! To create gaps you need to ask questions. This is a great time to visualise switching into The Coach Approach.

A coach stimulates the client's self-discovery by asking powerful questions.

Wearing Two Hats

To help you visualise the difference between accountant and coach when talking to clients, say, 'I'm going to take off my accountant hat and put on my advisor/coach hat. Is that okay?' This will help you switch into The Coach Approach.

In Step 7, you will most likely find that you need to prod, poke, encourage, and nudge some of the answers from your clients, particularly if they are introverts. The moment you ask them a question, their mind might go blank. As the advisor and facilitator, you need to have a great list of questions up your sleeve. I haven't left you hanging out to dry. Download the DIG Bonus Questions here to help you out: https://lyndasteffens.com/bonuses

As you're going through Step 7 with the client, refer back to the NOW analysis on the whiteboard for guidance on what questions to ask. That way, you'll probably think of some of your own questions. Refer to the DIG Bonus Questions as you need them.

Refer to all your tools – for example, the DIG Detailed Agenda, the client's completed interactive version of the BM model, and your notes from DISCOVER – to help prompt your client into thinking about what they need to do. For example, remind them that if they want to go from x out of 10 to 10 out 10 (point to the section on the whiteboard), or from a caterpillar to a butterfly (hold up the model, which should be on the desk in front of you), then you both need to get down to the nitty-gritty and look at the necessary changes to start moving towards that future.

Use everything you learned in Chapter 3 Time to DISCOVER, including using the big three questions, to help your client through the SWOT analysis:

1. What else?

2. If you did know what would it be?

3. How does that make you feel?

Remember: the Business Metamorphosis® model is there to use as an anchor throughout the DIG session if you need it. Refer to it to help prompt yourself with questions for your client. Use the three key stages – caterpillar, chrysalis, and butterfly, and the four key concepts – model, role, focus, and cashflow to keep you focused and on track.

I generally find a lot of action items come out of the SWOT analysis step, so be ready to capture them on the Action Plan. Remember: it doesn't matter whether they make the final cut or not. Your aim is to capture anything that even remotely smells like an action.

Okay, by this time, everyone will need a little break, most importantly your client. You'll have created quite a few gaps and countless questions in your client's mind so they'll be feeling a little bamboozled. Depending on the time of day, you might incorporate a snack like morning or afternoon tea in this break time.

Step 8 – FUTURE Analysis

All refreshed after your break, it's time to start wrapping things up and consolidating the gaps you've created thus far.

In strategic planning, referring to the future generally means 10 years from now because it's the optimum timeframe for taking action. It's not too short, so some goals can be realised, and not so long that the brain associates it with being too far into the future to be of any use. However, there is of course an exception and that is when the owner's age or circumstances involves a milestone that is less than 10 years away. The most common one concerns retirement, e.g. your client is 55 and wants to retire at 60; their factory lease runs out in eight years. Just be sure to check for these milestones before plotting the future out to 10 years.

You have perfectly prepped your client with all the information they need to consider broadly what they want their business to look like in the future. You've asked them some great questions and they're been on a rapid learning journey about their business future. Look at you go ...

 A coach is not an 'expert' but a facilitator of learning.

All you need to do in this step is complete with your client the FUTURE part of the 10 pieces of information from the NOW and FUTURE analysis grid. There is no need to go in order, in fact, it's better that you don't. Start with the easy stuff for the clients: fill in their age in 10 years' time and ask them how many hours they would like to be working then, what their role will be, how many weeks holidays they will be taking, what salary they want to be earning.

With these things filled in, your accounting brilliance now kicks in. You will be able to calculate what they would need to increase their net profit by in dollars if they want to earn a certain salary. Then, it's just a matter of deduction to work up through the gross profit to the turnover, completing the dollar amounts required and finally the percentage margins of each. You might also have some industry benchmarking figures available to help you out. Let that sink in with your client for a bit and then with this information guiding you, move onto a discussion around what services and products, clients and customers, staff and their roles would look like if the business was operating efficiently. All of these things will likely have to change/grow/morph in some way.

Don't forget to note down any actions that pop up out of this step.

Great job. Now let's bring it home.

Step 9 – The Gaps

Always refer to you and your client as 'we'. You're a team. There is no 'U' or 'I' in team.

Business Metamorphosis® showed your client a gap, DISCOVER showed them a gap, the NOW and FUTURE analysis showed them a gap, talking about their strategy and the realisation they didn't have an exit plan (or at least a solid one) showed them a gap, the SWOT analysis showed them gaps ... Using my system you have very expertly created a lot of gaps. Gaps you can help your client bridge.

Spend the next 10 minutes with your client investigating and discussing these gaps.

Start by saying, 'We want to go from here to here,' pointing to the x/10 and the 10/10, 'and from here to here,' pointing to the NOW and the FUTURE information on the board. 'How do we do that?'

'Clearly, we have some work to do. That's a great future so let's get a plan together and work out what's important from here. We won't have all the solutions today, that would be impossible, we just need a place to start.'

After reading this so far, you can imagine the robust discussion you will be right in the middle of. This is fabulous. It's exactly what you wanted. Your client might be a little bit flabbergasted and stunned by what you've shown them. Both are great signs that you have done a successful DIG session and you will feel it in the mood of the room.

Step 10 – Core Strategies and Priorities

At this point in the DIG session, it's a good idea to reassure your client how well they are doing. Just by looking around, they can see the mountains of information about their business you have been discussing. Point this out to them and let them know you haven't got much further to go. Say, 'We're going to be wrapping it up and getting some actions in place, but we've got to work out what things we need to tackle first.'

To help with setting priorities, start this step by going back to the SWOT analysis and ask your client to rate each item in terms of importance. For example, 'It's our No. 1 priority to get more customers. Of least concern is the new piece of equipment we would like to have, etc.'

Then discuss some strategies and actions around the top three priorities. Make sure you're including all these on your Action Plan.

This is also an excellent time to discuss data integrity and cashflow. As we all know, the key to great advisory work is having clean, correct, and timely data to work with. It's also very difficult, basically impossible, to grow any business that is insufficiently managing their cashflow. Data integrity and cashflow management will likely be the foundations of your basic DIG package. I discuss how to put together a basic DIG package a little later in the chapter.

Finally, move to prioritising all the Action Plan items. There's no need to reorder them. Wherever they are on the page, just use a simple numbering system to order the actions.

Step 11 – Leading Edge Business™ and Your Basic DIG Package

With everything now in order of priority, your client can clearly see they have a lot to get working on. They'll be wondering how on earth they're going to manage it on their own. Well, they're not, are they. Here's where Leading Edge Business™ and your basic DIG package come into play.

Reassure your client once again that today is not about finding all the answers, it's simply about finding a place to start and a way to move forward. You already have some ideas in place for that. Then move straight into a very brief introduction of Leading Edge Business™. And by brief I mean really brief. Your client will be suffering information overload at the end of the DIG session, so don't give them too much more to consider. The purpose of introducing Leading Edge Business™ is to show them that you have a plan and a system to help them move towards their FUTURE if they want further help from you. You could say something like, 'As you can see, we have a lot to do and your mind will be swimming with information right now, but I just wanted to show you how we might continue to work together going forward. We have an amazing and completely customisable system to work through when you're ready. Let me just show you quickly. When you're ready, we can chat about it in more detail. Today I just wanted to show you that we have everything in place to support you on your business journey. But first things first: let's talk about what we can do right now.'

Outline your basic DIG package. You've just stressed to them how important data integrity and cashflow management are for working towards their business future. It's an easy, simple, cost-effective place for them to start, one that could jeopardise future plans and initiatives if they don't get it right now and one way you can help them out immediately. Roll out to them your basic DIG package. Tell them what it includes and how much it will cost.

Tell them you can get a proposal out to them straightaway if they would like and that your team has availability to start immediately. Also, don't be afraid to customise it slightly for the client. They may wish to look at more services than the basic DIG package from the get-go. Just don't fall into the trap of offering too much too soon because if you confuse your client at this point, they will do nothing. I recommend you tell them that in your experience, this is what happens so you're going to help them take one step at a time.

Step 12 – Next Steps

The final DIG step involves transitioning into the third and final D, DELIVER.

Wrap up your DIG session by going back through the gaps and repeatedly reinforcing them.

- Start with Business Metamorphosis®

- Move to the DISCOVER business rating

- Then to the NOW and FUTURE analysis

- Summarise the SWOT analysis, the core strategies, priorities

- Finally the Action Plan.

Take photos of all the notes on butchers paper and the big sticky notes and offer them to the client to take with them if they would like to start working on their actions straightaway.

Let them know that within the next 24 hours, they'll receive an email with their Action Plan all nicely formatted and the proposal for the DIG package to approve.

If they have any questions, tell them to be sure to phone but that one of the team will be in touch in the next day or so to ask if they need any help.

And that's it, you're done, great job!

I love doing DIG sessions with my clients. They are rewarding and amazingly eye-opening for your clients. This is the work you love. Whatever you need to do so you can do more of it, do it!

Before the DIG Session

At the conclusion of your DISCOVER meeting with your client you would have booked the DIG. Your admin team would have issued an invoice for the DIG session and followed up with the client to pay before the session takes place. At the time of writing this book, I recommend charging a minimum of $1,650 (incl GST), but we'll talk more about pricing a bit further on because there are a couple of tricks to it.

A couple of days before the DIG, or at least the day before you want your admin team to confirm the DIG session with your client – the time and place, what they will need to bring –reassure your client that they don't need to prepare. Tell them the reason is that they are already experts in their business.

You'll see there are two DIG agendas. The DIG Detailed Agenda includes the 12 steps and is for you, the advisor. The DIG Client Agenda is a high-level overview of what you'll be covering. Send the DIG Client Agenda to the client when you confirm the DIG session. I'd recommend automating the initial confirmation in a standard email and then following up with a phone call.

With a new client, you may find they will need to bring in their financials, or allow you access to their accounting software. Most DIG sessions though will be with existing clients, so you'll have all their financial information to hand.

A DIG session is best done in your office, not at the client's premises. Business meetings at client's premises can be difficult due to distractions. It's too easy to be drawn into the day-to-day running of the business. If you don't have a suitable room at your office, you may wish to use a shared office facility with meeting rooms. There are loads of these flexi workspaces for hire in every town and city.

Make sure the room is fully prepped with water, notepads and pens, whiteboard, and butchers paper. I like to have the flexibility of taking notes in a variety of ways and find both a whiteboard and an easel with butchers paper works really well. There's always a lot more stuff to write down throughout the meeting than a standard whiteboard can hold. You don't want to be scrubbing notes off the whiteboard halfway through the meeting to fit more on. Extra-large sticky notes (in between A1 and A2 sized paper) are also handy. They're available from stationery providers all around the nation.

Of course, there's a DIG Meeting Template to structure your notetaking before the meeting. I recommend the following:

Task	Notetaking Medium
Now Analysis	Whiteboard
Future Analysis	Whiteboard
SWOT Analysis	Whiteboard
Current Strategy & Vision	Butchers paper / Sticky Notes
Core Strategies	Butchers paper / Sticky Notes
Action Plan	Butchers paper / Sticky Notes

It also helps to have the client's name and their DISCOVER business rating score out of 10 written in the top left-hand side of the whiteboard before you start. We'll get to why a little later on.

Use Your Tools

Make sure you have a copy of the Business Metamorphosis® model on hand. It will keep you focused, make you feel safe and secure, and give you the structure to have powerful client conversations that deliver consistent and meaningful messages.

Have a copy of the DIG Detailed Agenda, the client's completed interactive version of the BM model if they've already done one, and your notes from DISCOVER.

Action Plans for Meetings

DIG is the first meeting that requires an Action Plan. All meetings after DIG have action plans, even if it is an updated version of the previous meeting. Set up your Action Plan before the meeting so that you can add *anything* that remotely seems like an action. It doesn't matter if those actions make the final cut at the end of the meeting. The most important thing is that you capture them on the way through.

Action plans need detail:

a. What the action is – be clear and concise

b. When the action is to be completed by

c. Who is responsible for completing the action.

Action Plan		
Client Name:		
ACTION	DUE DATE	RESPONSIBILITY

Figure 4.1 Action Plan Template

Taking notes in a DIG session with clients is a great way to involve your team in joint meetings. It will also save you time in the long run. Choose the team member who will help you action the client's work as that way, they will already have a very good understanding of what's required without having to read the notes.

Finally, before the session starts, review your DISCOVER notes and the client's financials. The numbers will calm you and make you feel better. We're accountants ... we need to do what we need to do.

What to Include in Your Basic DIG Package

Data integrity, cashflow management, and basic financial KPIs are the areas you should be most concerned with if you wish to consistently start rolling out advisory services to your clients.

Data Integrity

One of the greatest challenges faced by the accounting industry today is the perceived efficiency gains supposedly brought about by the introduction of client accounting software. Most accountants if they honestly thought about it would realise they're more than likely taking longer to prepare a set of financials now using client data files than they did when they simply coded cheque and deposit books onto bank statements and entered the data from there.

Data integrity is a huge issue and what I believe to be one of the main reasons driving the rise of bookkeeping divisions in accounting practices. We all know the key to great advisory work is having clean, correct, and timely data to work with. Therefore, it stands to reason that the place to start with advisory offerings to most small businesses is the quality and timeliness of their data.

Data integrity services you may wish to consider in your basic DIG package include:

- Data file audit – find out what's wrong with the file

- Data file review and reset – fix what's wrong with the file

- Bookkeeping support and training – train how to keep the file in good working order

- Bookkeeping services – take over the bookkeeping on a regular basis.

Cashflow Management

Cash is the lifeblood of business. Without it not much happens. Certainly no growth initiatives or plans can be undertaken and to be brutally honest, without it your clients cannot afford to pay for your advisory services. Consequently, helping and showing clients how to manage their cashflow is in the long term a very noble cause.

Cashflow management services you may wish to consider in your basic DIG package include:

- Cashflow budget preparation – including entry in client's data file

- Cashflow management monthly phone call – monitor cashflow levels monthly.

KPIs

An understanding of basic financial KPIs like turnover, gross profit, and net profit margins is a great place to start educating business owners on the financial wellbeing of their business. If you've already prepared the cashflow budget, then monitoring and tracking these three basic financial KPIs will be easy.

Financial KPI services you may wish to consider in your basic DIG package include:

- Financial KPI monthly tracking and phone call – monitor and track basic KPIs.

If you've already set up a regular cashflow management phone call, the financial KPI discussion will only add another five to 10 minutes to the conversation. Build a simple email template that incorporates the key data. Perhaps add in a simple graph or two. You can train your admin team to put this together and send to the client. Your follow-up will be the scheduled monthly phone call.

In the monthly phone call, make sure you are sticking to just monitoring and tracking cashflow flow and the KPIs. For a more robust discussion, you may wish to offer your client the more advanced Leading Edge Business™ solutions. Don't fall into the trap of giving away advice for free. It's easily done.

Bear in mind that the basic DIG package is just the starting point for advisory services for your client. You want to be able to leverage up as time goes on. This is one of the selling points for your clients. They can dip their toe in the water and it allows you to keep their costs down in the initial stages of their advisory journey.

A Word on Pricing Your Basic DIG Packages

You want to ease your client into monthly commitments, so start off small. Perhaps the data file audit, data file reset and review, and preparation of a cashflow budget are one-off upfront costs. Clients are more likely to accept one-off costs, which have a clear beginning and end, than monthly ongoing fees. To start monthly fees off small, you could wrap together a monthly data file review (only reviewing the month's transactions), cashflow management phone call, and bookkeeping support into a smaller monthly fee. I think this would be a great way to get clients started on the advisory journey. Starting off small will also give your clients time to trust the process so they don't have the feeling you're trying to get them to jump in feet first right from the get-go.

These are all only suggestions. You may have your own ideas about what you would like to build into your basic DIG package. Your client base may have an entirely different set of needs so just take it slowly and introduce services to them over time.

Pricing a DIG Session

And finally, pricing the actual DIG session. On confirmation of the meeting, your admin team would have created and sent an invoice to the client for the DIG session. But how much should you charge? My recommendation at the time of writing this book is a minimum of $1,650 incl GST.

This price recommendation is for a DIG session where you have allowed two to three hours with one to two clients in the room, say a husband and wife team. If you're involving any more people than that, perhaps another family member, a senior team member, or sometimes the client's whole team, then the pricing needs to change. I often do DIG sessions with the whole team when working with accounting firms. It's a great way to engage the team right from the start of the process.

You need to allow more time to complete DIG sessions with more people in the room. The difficulty level goes up so you need to bring all your facilitator skills to the table to keep it on track. More people mean more ideas and more things to say, so it takes longer to complete. You might like to allow three to four hours for these sessions, no more than four hours because that is the limit of your client's concentration. The value you generate starts to slip proportionately with your client's concentration. For these larger and more difficult DIG sessions, I recommend starting from $3,300 incl GST at the time of writing this book.

Congratulations! You've made it through another of the huge implementation chapters. Just one more to go. The next chapter affords you some much needed lighter reading, so enjoy that and take a well-earned breather.

After reading all of this, I bet you're freaking out, right?

It's all good, keep calm and keep reading. We're about to deal with the freak-outs to calm your nerves.

Freak-out Number One

I'll wager you're thinking, hang on, just hang on, I'm not an expert in every client's business, how on earth am I supposed to know what my client needs to do to go from their NOW to their FUTURE?

And you're absolutely right; you won't know. That's the expert in you talking! You're not an expert in every client's business and neither should you try to be. In this process you're their advisor.

A coach is not an 'expert' but a facilitator of learning.

The advisor/coach approach is very different from that of an expert. Advisors ask, experts tell. Experts function very well in the compliance space. Advisory offerings are different. The reason you've found it so hard to date is because you've been approaching it with an expert mindset.

Facilitating not Participating

You're asking questions, not providing answers.

You won't know the answers.

You work with your client and together, develop the strategies, priorities, and actions that need to be undertaken. The client is the expert in their business, not you. You help and guide them to the answers.

A coach stimulates clients' self-discovery by asking powerful questions.

Freak-out Number Two

Clients won't pay $1,650 for this!

Yes, they will, and happily so. Read back through the 12 steps and look at the value you're giving them. It's a bargain for $1,650 and your client will feel that way too. If you've followed the system, introduced them to Business Metamorphosis®, and carried out a DISCOVER meeting with them, they absolutely will pay that amount for the DIG session. You will have already created sufficient gaps in the client's mind for them to want to know more. What's more, they will already suspect that you are the solution to bridging those gaps.

Freak-out Number Three

Every business is different and will need different solutions. How can you know beforehand what your basic DIG package should look like and how much it should cost?

I want you to just think for a minute. How many business owners started their business because they hated it and weren't very good at it? NONE! Almost all small business owners end up in business because they are great at what they do, even accountants! Often, what they lack when starting out in business are the knowledge and skills to run the business. The skillset needed to run a business is very different from the skills required to just do what they do.

This same principle can be applied from one business owner to another. As an accountant, you have business skills and knowledge in abundance. You might not always apply them to your own businesses but you have them nonetheless. You see it every single day in the clients you talk to and the work you do that just some business basics would go a long way to helping small business owners with successful business management. It's these basics that you can incorporate into your basic DIG package.

I understand you might still be feeling a little overwhelmed with everything in this chapter. There's a lot to take in. If you still feel you need a little more help, go to my website https://lyndasteffens.com and check out when my next Business Metamorphosis® workshop is. Just like DISCOVER, we spend at least half a day on how to run a DIG session, and on the mechanics of the DIG session, and we take time to practise running the sessions.

Make sure you complete the actions at the end of this chapter. They're short, sharp, and will keep your implementation on track. Most of all, keep reading and everything will fall into place if it hasn't already.

Actions to Take After Reading This Chapter

1. Download the DIG agendas.
2. Download the DIG invoice wording.
3. Build a basic DIG solution using the advisory service lists you completed in Chapter 1 Sex Lies and Revolution and the product build template.

Additional Information/Resources

- DIG Client Agenda

- DIG Detailed Agenda

- DIG Invoice wording

- NOW and FUTURE Analysis Grid

- DIG Product Build Template

You will find the links to download all the documents listed under the above two headings here: https://lyndasteffens.com/bonuses

Okay, that's the end of DIG. Let's get on to our third and final D, DELIVER.

5

Time to DELIVER

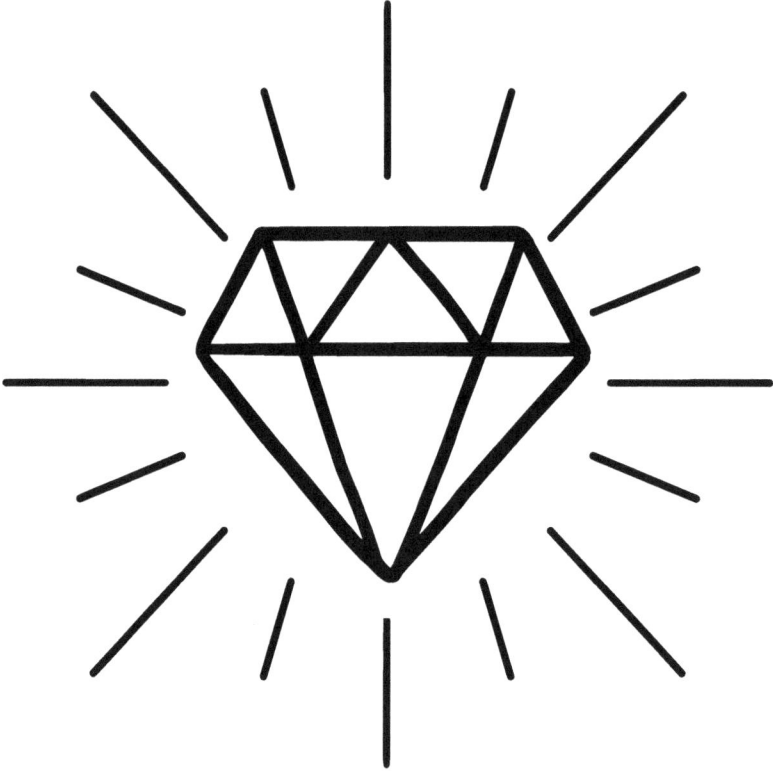

Always deliver more than expected

— Larry Page[10]

---

10 Goodreads.com, 2019

The third and final D, DELIVER, brings it all together. Take the time to implement the process by automating and standardising, always following up with clients, and you'll find this final D is the simplest but most powerful of the three.

DELIVER is the process of providing a client a proposal that shows both the timeframe and the delivery cost of everything you have discussed thus far. There is no need to show you how to put together a client proposal. You already know how to do that.

Just remember: if you don't deliver, or you don't deliver quickly enough, the time you have taken as an advisor to build confidence, trust, and rapport with your client may be lost. You don't want to jeopardise advisory offerings with current clients and affect possible future advisory referral sources. This will put you back on the very slippery slope of an increasing reliance on compliance. As you now know, being firmly stuck on the reliance on compliance treadmill will not bring you sustainable business success in the long term.

Don't let your hard work up to now go to waste. Leverage the gaps you've created with your client as you've stepped through Business Metamorphosis®, DISCOVER, and DIG. Build on the value proposition you've established by using these powerful processes, with no fear of surprising your client with unexpected pricing outcomes. You will have already set up an expectation of the monthly fee to roll out their action plans so it will not be a surprise to them.

You will never know unless you offer, so take advantage of the opportunities and use the power of the upsell. Failing to ask clients what they want from advisors is one of the major stumbling blocks to delivering advisory services successfully. If you think about it, the arrogance of the expert mindset of self-assessing what you think clients want has only served to enhance the conundrum. As an advisor, the decision is not up to you. Your client will happily accept, or not accept, the options you provide them in expectation of the future value you have created.

Keep your client's confidence in your abilities as an advisor on the up and up by delivering and following up on what you have said you would do, and do it quickly.

Did you know that seven out of 10 accounting firms surveyed described client fee negotiations as challenging, or very challenging?

> *The perfect ending to any day, race or project is to finish strong*
> — *Gary Ryan Blair*[11]

Here are my three simple steps to DELIVER quickly and effortlessly.

Step 1: Automate, Automate, Automate

Now let's be clear when I say automate. I don't necessarily mean you need to use technology.

You may be familiar with Tim Ferriss' 2007 book *The 4-Hour Work Week* and if you're not I recommend reading it. Tim talks about Automating, Delegating, and Eliminating as the three basic principles for being more effective in your day. The overall premise is that if you multiplied your effectiveness by 10, you could condense a full work week into just four hours.

Automate means the simple act of developing checklists, standard procedures, and in the case of client proposals, standard paragraphs. These are all straightforward and uncomplicated ways of automation. You probably already have standard paragraphs for service offerings in your system somewhere, but I bet you don't use them. You know, the paragraphs you go searching for every time you do another fee? To get you started, I've made available my DELIVER Standard Opening Paragraph that you can use to start all your

---

11 BrainyQuote, 2019

proposals with. Just grab it from the member-only bonuses section on my website: https://lyndasteffens.com/bonuses

When formulating your standard paragraphs, make sure to include a pricing guide with each one. In fact, you started this process right back in Chapter 1 Sex Lies and Revolution, so grab out those lists and get working on them.

Now, I know you're thinking, 'I can't put a price on each service because each client will need a different level of each service.' And you're right! To tackle this, you just need to use a 'starting from' fee for each service and then add pricing bands, e.g. small, medium, and large OR basic, standard, complex ... something like that. Based on your current client base, you determine what the definition of each of these pricing bands is. Client factors that you may like to consider would be their turnover level, the number of staff they have, or a rating of their business complexity. It's up to you. Remember: standard paragraphs and pricing don't need to be perfect. They're not set in stone for the rest of your life, you can change them, so don't get bogged down in the detail. Just get started with something. Each service may be priced differently. Some may be one-off fees, for example, preparing a cashflow budget, but others may be a monthly ongoing fee, for example, monitoring monthly actual to budgeted results and meeting to discuss these.

Failing to take the time to standardise and automate simple tasks like this costs big time in the DELIVERY phase. Don't let this happen. Hand over the task to your admin team and have them compile and/or tidy up your standard paragraphs. Then, if you choose to implement technology, you have a clean and consistent set of standard paragraphs to put into operation.

Moving along, if you choose to incorporate technology in DELIVER with the view to enhancing your automation, then do so with caution. When technology is not set up correctly, is not used as intended, or is in unskilled hands, it can have disastrous effects on effectiveness and productivity and be a real hazard for timely delivery. Don't get me wrong. There is some amazing proposal generation software out there which will take automation to the next level. Just don't be fooled. You (or your admin team) MUST take the time to set it up correctly in order to execute it in a way that saves time in the long run.

A Word on Technology

Shovels don't dig holes, and proposal software solutions and project management/workflow solutions will not do the job for you.

If you'd like to go ahead with these, make sure you allow plenty of implementation time to get the systems up and running. I can't stress this enough.

If you've been doing your action items at the end of each chapter, then you will have already put together your basic DIG package. Once standardised, it can be put into a client proposal at a moment's notice.

Step 2: Follow Up, Follow Up, Follow Up

Following up and staying in touch with your client from the start of DELIVER all the way through until the proposal is accepted is non-negotiable, so you need to find a way to make this happen.

A word of warning. I know that as accountants, we feel the same way about following up as we do about sales: urrgghhhh, right? We feel this way because it's not instinctive for us, we struggle to see the importance of it, and we don't do it ... WHAT? ... Didn't I just say it was non-negotiable and you had to make it happen? Absolutely I did, but maybe you're not the best person for the job. Think about it for a second.

Get your admin team involved. In fact, DELIVER is the step that they should own. Empower them to take control of the third and final D and engage them fully in the process. Have them track the proposal and make all initial follow-ups via email, text, and/or phone call. They'll know when a client needs to speak with you further and will be able to schedule a time for you to make that call, a time suitable for both you and the client so they have your undivided attention. There's no need for you to be making the initial follow-ups, just so long as someone is.

The timeliness of following up is also key to delivering successfully, so set some standard response times and expectations for your team. I would suggest the following:

Time	Follow-Up	Medium	Responsibility
Proposal sent	Advise proposal sent and how to accept it. 'We are keen to get started on delivering your 10 out of 10 business.'	Phone call	Admin
24 hrs after proposal sent	Check they have received and were able to access the proposal. Do they have any questions?	SMS	Admin
3–5 days after proposal sent	Check they reviewed the proposal. Would they like to schedule a quick catch-up call with the advisor? 'We want to start helping you realise your business future.'	Phone call	Admin
5 days after proposal sent	See heading below 'The Advisor Follow-Up' for suggested content.	Phone call	Advisor
Proposal unsuccessful	Ensure your client is receiving your monthly newsletter and further marketing content about Business Metamorphosis® and Leading Edge Business™.	Email	Admin/Marketing

The admin follow-ups only need to be a couple of lines and should be standardised scripts. That way, the same message is conveyed to every client in the same way.

The Advisor Follow-Up

The advisor follow-up cannot be scripted as it will be different for every client, but I recommend following the standard process set out below.

1. Prepare: Take five minutes to prepare for your follow-up phone call. Ensure you have all your tools at hand and review the notes from DISCOVER and DIG.

2. Proposal Enquiry: Firstly, enquire how the client is going with the proposal. Have they opened and reviewed it?

3. Proof: Review the rating they gave their business in DISCOVER and talk to them about taking their business from the x out of 10 to the 10 out of 10 they're dreaming of. Utilise the powerful combination of the good and bad words you gathered in the DISCOVER meeting.

4. Query: Ask your client what their concerns are. Let them know you're eager to help them get started on their business journey. If you need to adjust the services, the timing of the service, the wording or the pricing in the proposal, then do so. Better to adjust the proposal and have the opportunity to work with your client than not to work with them. Be careful of discounting. For the most part, this will not work. If you've followed the process up until now, the value proposition you have put in place will do the work for you and discounting won't be required.

 **Facilitating not Participating**

You're asking questions, not providing answers.

You won't know the answers.

 **Out of your Comfort Zone**

Yes, this is new, yes, this is different, yes, it is foreign to you, and yes, it will take practice and effort.

Step 3: Accept and Celebrate, Celebrate, Celebrate

When the proposal is accepted, celebrate a job well done. We don't celebrate enough of the small things and celebration sends team engagement through the roof. Message or email the team, announce it at your morning meetings, ring a bell, bang a drum, tell your spouse, tell someone even if it's just the cat, acknowledge your success.

I've just realised I suggest talking to your cat and using your cat as a practice client quite a bit. I don't have a cat, I'm more of a dog person. I wonder if accountants as a group have a preferred animal companion. I might have it all wrong. Maybe I should be suggesting you talk to your fish, bird, or guinea pig. For a bit of fun perhaps I will do a survey.

Back to celebrate. A great idea is for you and your team to track the conversion rate of advisory proposals, and set a conversion rate goal with reward at the end for motivation. Then get to scheduling the work and client meetings. This is where the magic begins, and where doing more of the work you and your team loves becomes a reality.

Why Admin is So Important to DELIVER

The trick with DELIVER is to get admin involved and engaged in the process. Unlike the advisor, they are not emotionally connected to the success or failure of the process so they are central to DELIVER.

Involve admin in the initial planning stages of the project and keep them in the loop. Fill them in on what you're trying to achieve overall. Give them the big picture and have them track and report on the conversion rate goal you set in Step 3 (Accept and Celebrate, Celebrate, Celebrate). You might not know it, but you may have just taken the first steps to becoming a business butterfly yourself.

After your client's DIG session, admin will have collated the notes and filed all relevant documents and information in the client file. With your basic DIG package already in place and the standardised advisory paragraphs you've created for DELIVER, it should be easy to develop a proposal tick and flick checklist that you can complete after the DIG session with your client. You'll use this to convey to your admin team the services you would like to offer the client so they can complete the initial draft of the DELIVER proposal. Once that initial draft is complete, you review it, request changes if required, approve it, and admin can send it, follow up, and monitor from there.

DELIVER proposals don't need to be perfect. You'll find that clients want to get cracking. You don't want to keep them waiting. Don't forget to include good, better, and best options (see below). If you never offer, you'll never know.

Good, Better and Best Options

In the previous chapter, we talked about the basic DIG option and that for most businesses this starts with data integrity services like bookkeeping audits, basic bookkeeping training and ongoing bookkeeping, cashflow budgets, simple monitoring, and business basics. This basic DIG package is a good place to get started with advisory services.

Your better option may be to take the basic DIG package and wrap up the client's compliance needs into one simple, easy monthly payment. Great for their cashflow, great for your cashflow, WIN-WIN!

And your best option would be to roll out the Leading Edge Business™ program with your client. Leading Edge Business™ builds on the gap in DIG, kicks off with a strategic planning session, and then moves into regular monthly advisory meetings that follow a set path. It's an extremely powerful process and one we discuss in detail in the upcoming chapters.

Monthly Meetings with Your Clients

These don't need to be at your office or at your client's premises. Think about using an internet-based meeting platform like Zoom or Skype that work well across a number of devices including computers, laptops, tablets, and smart phones. This means you can work from anywhere and so can your client. It saves travel time and parking, keeps disruption to daily schedules to a minimum, and makes attending the meetings convenient and easy.

Once DELIVER is implemented it is designed to be super-slick, quick, and easy. It's just a matter of putting together the proposal, sending it out, and following it up in a quick turnaround time.

To wrap up:

Get Admin Involved

Whether you're using technology or not to deliver quick turnaround times of 24 hours or less for proposals, you'll need assistance.

Implementation of Technology Takes Time

Don't incorporate technology into DELIVER unless you are 100% committed to taking the time to implement it correctly. Plan what you need it to do, how it will interact with your other software, and who's responsible for each part of the process. Work with software providers to implement successfully.

Follow Up

Always follow up with a client after sending the DELIVER proposal. Using a combination of you, your admin team, and technology automation will make this process efficient.

After reading everything in this chapter you might have a number of warning bells going off in your mind. Things like:

'It's impossible to get a proposal out in less than 24 hours.'

No, it's not if you're prepared. If you have automated and standardised your paragraphs and pricing and have your admin involved, you will have no trouble turning around a proposal in 24 hours. Make sure you schedule your appointments and meetings appropriately, so you give yourself sufficient time to complete any notes from your DIG meeting, complete the proposal tick and flick, and review the client proposals. Don't let yourself be the bottleneck in the process.

You might also be thinking, 'How will I know good, better, and best options for every single client? It'll take me ages to work these out.'

You have already gathered all the information you need in DIG. You have your basic DIG solution already prepared. You'll get quicker at wrapping compliance solutions into monthly packages as you go along, and the introduction of the Leading Edge Business™ is standard. You have nothing to work out.

'What if I don't have time to follow up?'

Well, I'm here to tell you, you need to make time. Step 2 in DELIVER is non-negotiable. Automation and your admin team will be a godsend for following up. Give them the permission and they will make it happen. Give yourself enough time to review proposals in your schedule, and you must also make time to follow up with clients. Manage your time efficiently and ensure you're not the reason DELIVER fails. Set standard booking schedules. For example, if a DIG meeting is booked in your calendar, ensure both proposal review and follow-up slots are also allocated.

Well, that's the third and final D complete. Don't forget to stop and complete the actions at the end of the chapter before moving on. Take your time. Rome wasn't built in a day.

Actions to Take After Reading This Chapter

1. Write a standard paragraph including pricing for your 'good' option (basic DIG package).

2. Write a standard opening paragraph for your 'better' option (inclusion of compliance).

3. Schedule regular time in your diary over the next couple of weeks to write standard paragraphs and pricing for other advisory services.

Additional Information/Resources

• DELIVER Standard Opening Paragraph

You will find the links to download all the documents listed under the above two headings here: https://lyndasteffens.com/bonuses

6

Find Your Superpowers

Success is achieved by developing our strengths, not by eliminating our weaknesses

— Marilyn Von Savant[12]

---

12 Goodreads.com, 2019

Being different in the accounting industry is actually a good thing. Stepping outside of your comfort zone takes courage. Arm yourself with knowledge, take the time you need, and be motivated to objectively understand yourself. It is only then that you will find your superpowers, the place where your true power and value lie. It's in this place that your ability to forge ahead with change is strengthened and magnified.

Join the revolution and help me reverse those worldwide business failure statistics. Become an accountant who does not have to worry about the future but instead tackles it head on with your newly found superpowers and knowledge.

Once you understand what makes you tick and how this affects your working relationships, you have the power to change it and get on with doing the best possible job for your client. By talking about more than just tax and accounting with your clients, you'll connect with them like never before. Make visits to your office something your clients value, something they want to do, something they may even enjoy, rather than something they wish they could avoid and that fills them with dread.

Remember: your number one job is to support your clients on their business journey, not drown them in tax and accounting facts and figures.

Learn to love sales by taking a different approach and viewing it differently. It won't even feel like selling because you'll be doing what comes naturally to you – helping your clients. Just by changing your conversations, be confident that you're delivering and expressing value in everything you do, giving your clients what they want and value.

You'll see how the systems in this book complement and boost your natural talents, not fight against them. Embrace the butterfly effect and see how small changes can have huge impacts.

Did you know that 78% of accounting employees recently surveyed agreed that greater skills, diversity, and innovation are the keys to increasing team capabilities?

> *Whether you think you can, or you think you can't, you're right*
>
> — *Henry Ford*[13]

The Real Accountant

The Real Accountant is a term I have coined to describe the person behind the professional mask.

As an industry we've conditioned ourselves to think that to be professional is to be an expert, to know the right answers. Hiding behind complicated accounting and tax legislation, we're in control, while bearing the brunt of jokes about 'bean counters' with no personality, and shielding ourselves from clients to make us feel safe.

Throughout my career there have been plenty of times I've felt out of place and misunderstood, and I'm sure you have too. I'm letting you know that it is far safer to just be yourself. Follow your natural instincts and embrace the Real Accountant. Let's rip away that professional mask and explore what I've learned about who the Real Accountant is.

I've spent a good part of the last 10 years researching this. I wanted to know what drives us, what our natural instincts are, and how we can be the best we can be, so I can help other accountants see their true value.

If we've let ourselves believe that we can't offer advisory services just because we've failed to implement them consistently in the past, we need to realise that it's because we've been going about it

---

13 https://addicted2success.com/quotes/38-memorable-henry-ford-quotes

all wrong. We can do advisory services. Our previous difficulties in implementing them have rocked our perceived value to the core. If we don't value what we do, then how are our clients going to? Accountants have the ability to change lives. Yes, you, the humble accountant. We need to stop underestimating ourselves and understand truly where our value lies.

Our clients are our number one motivator. We're service people and we're happiest when we're making a real difference to our clients' lives. In my experience, accountants take great pride in client service and looking after clients. That's one of the reasons we're so good at giving away our knowledge and advice.

Several years back just at the start of my consulting journey, a business associate asked me for some advice. They had substantial debt owing to creditors, including to the Australian Tax Office (ATO), with whom their accountant was helping them negotiate a settlement deal. The accountant was also one of their creditors and was owed a substantial sum, yet they were continuing to assist their client. Their accountant had made a recommendation to accept the current ATO offer and my associate wasn't certain of the accountant's motivations, thinking they might just be trying to scare them into settling to get their account paid. I reassured them that the accountant was not trying to scare them, that that was not how accountants roll.

I've seen accountants go to the wall to help clients, put business partnerships on the line, and risk tens of thousands of dollars in fees, trying to help clients out of some awful financial situations, so I was 100% confident that the accountant was not scaring them unnecessarily. I told my business associate that accountants have a measured and conservative approach and if their accountant was telling them they needed to take the offer, then they should do so.

Your Superpowers Detailed

The same as with all superheroes, your superpowers come with great responsibility. You must promise to use them for good, not evil, and swear an oath of allegiance to me for helping you realise what they are. Now, raise your right hand and repeat after me … just kidding, no oath of allegiance, but using your powers for good, not evil, is a given.

In the introduction I mentioned that people attracted to the accounting industry, and accountants in particular, have a distinct profile. Let's now look at this profile in detail.

Have I caught you skim-reading yet? I bet you are, because this is a touchy-feely fluffy chapter. Nothing technical or process driven in here, right? Be careful you don't let your expert mindset determine what you should and should not read, because I cannot stress enough how important it is to read this chapter.

Guess what? You have superpowers and you didn't even know it. There are quite a few of them, so let's get cracking.

Superpower No. 1: Information

We are information nuts. We love data, and the more detailed the better. We like to understand in detail what we're up against and we're not happy to move forward with anything or make a decision unless we have researched and gained as much information as we can beforehand.

Think about a time when you felt pressured to make a decision quickly. It was most likely very stressful for you. You felt as though you didn't have enough information or time to make your decision properly.

To research and gather all this information we value so much takes time, especially to do it properly and in the detail we require.

We value information so highly that we don't factor time into the equation at all. It's irrelevant, it will take as long as it needs to.

How many times have you answered the question, 'How long will that take?' by responding with something like, 'It will be done when I'm finished'? How many times have you been frustrated with your team when they've done the same thing? Sound familiar? Yet, our industry is built on a time-based costing system to measure value. Seems a little crazy, huh!

Our information superpower sets us up perfectly to operate in the accounting industry, which involves a mammoth amount of information from a vast sum of sources of highly specific, detailed, and technical information and the application of such. In a nutshell, we're perfect for what we do, but ... and you knew there'd be a but... there's a flipside. Ever heard the saying our greatest strength is our greatest weakness? Well, it's true.

We value information so much and won't do anything without it, so everyone else in the world must also, right? Wrong. I'm sure you'll recall talking to someone, not necessarily a client because this will happen in your personal life as well, and you see this person start to roll their eyes, maybe yawn, jiggle their feet, or become downright fidgety. That's when you know your information superpower has taken over and is crushing the evil on the other side of your desk ... but wait, they're not your enemy. You shouldn't be doing that to them. Remember what I said about promising to use your superpowers for good and not evil? Here's where it kicks in.

You need to be aware of your information superpower and how to use it effectively. Most clients won't love information as much as you do. That's why they come to you. They expect you've got it covered. They don't need you to tell them all about it. They're just cool that you know. That is why understanding your superpowers and the self-awareness to use them properly is so important.

Superpower No. 2: Analysis

Your analysis superpower complements your information superpower. We research and collect so much information we'd be in real trouble if we had no way to organise, store, and analyse that data. We have a supercharged ability to use systems, processes, and procedures to sort, manage, and analyse all our information. Think about it. When you go out for dinner with a group and you can't split the bill, who do they ask to work out who owes what? You, right?

But buyer beware. Here comes the responsibility and awareness bit again. Because we're very good at putting together, organising, and analysing data quickly, this makes us very prone to overcomplicating things. We can handle it, but for the most part our clients cannot.

They will become extremely frustrated if you try to download masses of information and explain how it all fits together. Be aware of this and use your superpower for good.

Superpower No. 3: Low Risk

A key component of our distinct accounting profile is that we tend towards being risk averse or low risk. We are very much of the mindset that if it ain't broke, don't fix it.

I bet you'll have used this little beauty in an argument against change a few times before, am I right? Change doesn't come easy to humans in general but notably, it does not come easy to those with a low-risk profile.

This superpower allows us to be conservative and measured in most things we do. It's exactly what our clients want us to be when we're helping them with financial and business decisions. They don't want somebody who's going to jump on the latest bandwagon or sail uncharted waters that will throw them into crazy business situations full of risk. As accountants, we're simply not going to do that, in fact we're going to use the full force of all our superpowers together and take the time to gather the information we need, analyse it, and then take a measured approach to arrive at the best result for our client. Our clients know this. It's exactly why they trust us and have been hanging around us for so long. Now, they want us to take it to another level.

It's possible for those of us with a low-risk profile to change. You can do anything you want to do. But let me share with you the fundamental components that I've learned make change much more palatable for accounting types. I call it my secret sauce recipe for change.

In fact, I run a full-day workshop exclusively designed for accountants and introverts dedicated to making the most of your day. It's called Power up your Potential, and we work through my seven strategies for overcoming ineffectiveness. The secret sauce recipe for change is the second strategy, which is based on all the knowledge I've gathered about accountants and what makes us tick.

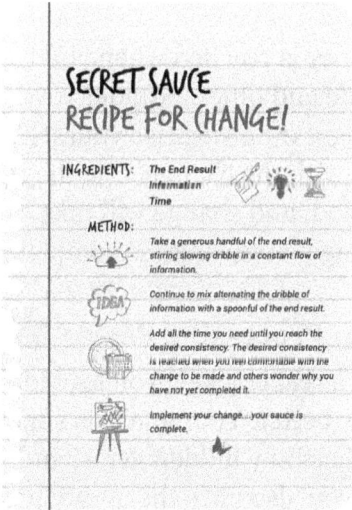

Figure 6.1 Secret Sauce Recipe for Change

As you can see from the figure above, you only need three ingredients: The End Result, Information, and Time. You start with a generous handful of the End Result. Always starting with the end in mind is not only a very effective strategy but it allows your third superpower – low risk – to play out to its full extent. You like to know what is in front of you, what you're trying to achieve, and to limit the number of surprises going forward if you can.

Stirring slowly, dribble in a constant flow of Information, your No. 1 and most prominent superpower. Without it, you're not going to budge a millimetre.

Continue to mix, alternating the dribble of Information with a spoonful of the End Result. This step in the method gives time for your Superpower No. 2 to kick in. You'll organise, sort, and analyse all the information given to you with the End Result, and debate the pros and cons as you continue to mix up your secret sauce.

Add all the Time you need until you reach the desired consistency. Superpowers No. 1, 2, and 3 all need a decent amount of Time. When it comes to change, it's a longer game for you, so take all the Time you need to ensure success.

The desired consistency is reached when you feel comfortable with the change to be made and others wonder why you have not yet completed it. You might even surprise yourself how quickly you become comfortable with the change. Use the right ingredients, understand the method, and change will take care of itself. Implement your change. Your sauce is complete.

Superpower No. 4: Processing Power

Superpower No. 4 is a real cracker. You love lots of information and the more detailed the better. Your analysis superpower keeps it all organised and deciphers any hidden gems, and you're measured and conservative. But ... you also have the ability to solve complex issues and problems in your head.

You don't need to doodle, draw, build, touch, listen, see, or hear. You just think and the solutions come to you. Your mind is a processing powerhouse and I wager you've often wondered, quite innocently

I might add, why you seem to be three steps in front of everyone else. Am I right? You've already come up with a solution and are moving onto possible improvements while everyone else is still back fumbling around looking for the first answer. Seeing this superpower in action boggles the minds of others, but you've taken it for granted all this time. This superpower makes you extremely solution-focused and once again makes you super-qualified to undertake the work you do, whether that's compliance or advisory work.

Here's the rub with Superpower No. 4. While all this solving of problems, devising solutions, and processes are going on in your mind, you often don't listen to what others are saying. You're too busy processing, delivering the solution, and thinking you know what's best. I address this a little later in the chapter when we talk about active listening.

However, leveraging and developing your processing power superpower will be a driving force in rolling out advisory services to your clients. Think about it. Introverts like to process things internally. It suits us. So embrace your superpower and turn it on full throttle. Don't be afraid of little patches of silence in meetings, particularly if you just say, 'Let me think on that for a second.' Clients will know exactly what you're doing – coming up with the next amazing question.

A coach stimulates clients' self-discovery by asking powerful questions.

Superpower No. 5: Love of Learning

In my experience, accountants are high achievers and knowledge superstars and I'm sure you are no different. Look at all your superpowers. When used together, they make you one powerful superhero. You seek out information and have an almost insatiable appetite to learn. This love of learning is precisely why the work you love to do is advisory based. When you're given the freedom of not being expected to know the answers, all your superpowers kick in, particularly your love of learning to explore your client's business and investigate how to help them deliver their business future.

Your Value

Your value to all those around you is not in answers. It is clearly and undeniably in questions.

With great power, comes great responsibility
— *Spider-Man[14]*

Just like Spider-Man, you should accept the responsibility of your superpowers, not only using them for good and not evil but exercising them, keeping them in tip-top shape, developing them and honing them to be as effective as they can be. Embrace the Real Accountant, play to your strengths and be objective about your limits, use your superpowers and take responsibility for developing them.

The Real Accountant

Never stop learning and growing as a person. It's key to your success and happiness. Embrace the Real Accountant.

Every superhero and superhero story has a nemesis. There's always a villain in the story sent to test the superhero and challenge them at every corner, every which way they turn. Superman had Lex Luthor, Thor had Loki, Batman had The Joker, and accountants have teachers. Whoops, did I actually write that? It's a bit naughty. My apologies, teachers, but you do test us out and I'm sure you have felt the same way about accountants many times over. Thank goodness you do test us out. We celebrate you for challenging us. I'm taking

---

14 Quotes.net, 2019

the punt that few teachers will read this book, so let's keep this between ourselves, okay?

The point I'm making at the expense of our teaching friends is that all these adversaries challenge the superhero and their superpowers. Close your eyes and imagine for a second the villain taunting the superhero from afar, waggling their fingers at them and saying, 'Just try to catch me, I bet you can't.' They throw down the gauntlet and dare you to be better. Are you ready to pick up that gauntlet and run with it? It gives you the most wonderful opportunity to prove yourself. Understand the extent and limits of your superpowers. Be brave and ask how you can do better. Hone your skills and enjoy the challenge.

Tips for Honing Those Superpowers

Storytelling

Incorporate storytelling into your every day. Let me tell you a story about my storytelling journey.

The first time I stood up in front of a group of professional accountants, I was speaking at a local CPA professional development event. I was pretty nervous to say the least but I had everything planned out and knew what I wanted to say. I started my presentation with a personal story about me and why I love what I do. After my story, I repeated my introduction: 'Hello, I'm Lynda Steffens, I'm an accountant and an introvert.'

Introducing myself as an accountant and an introvert quite obviously struck a chord with the audience because the whole room went silent. I'm a keen observer of people and I've honed this storytelling skill over the last few years to a fine art, but I didn't need to observe people to notice their reaction at this moment. It was one of those true mike-drop moments and I don't think I had truly realised the power of storytelling until then.

Storytelling is part of human evolution. From our earliest ancestors until now, stories have been used as a way of passing down important survival lessons about gathering food, finding shelter, developing tools, leaving the sleeping sabre-toothed tiger alone, and so on.

You may be thinking, 'That's all well and good, Lynda, but you're talking about using stories in accounting. Accountants don't tell stories.'

Ahh, you are right, accountants don't normally tell stories, but my goodness you should. You can rely on the same inherent capacity to learn through stories that your ancestors used for survival. Except this time, it's not survival in a prehistoric world but survival in a modern, global business world. The principles are the same. You can use storytelling to strategically communicate vital information to your clients, ensuring their business growth and success.

Research tells us that the great stories that get remembered and that pass the test of time are those with specific detail rather than abstract. If you think about cavemen, if they only gave wishy-washy details about where to find food, the results could have been disastrous. Using precise details in a story, describing the people, the objects, and the events, grabs people's attention because you're engaging their brains and activating sensory memories.

And low and behold, your No. 1 Superpower, Information, is all about detail, so storytelling is right up your alley. Stories in a business sense don't need to be funny. You don't need to make people laugh or cry, you just need to be able to explain things in detail using a story format. It's a much better approach to educating your clients than just bombarding them with facts and figures.

Instead of going straight to the hardcore facts and figures, tell a story and build authentic and emotional connections with your clients through storytelling.

How to Get Started with Storytelling

Storytelling is just recounting a previous event or situation using real-life examples to illustrate a point and encourage certain actions or behaviours. You might change names or not use them at all. Change the situation slightly if you need as long as it gets the point across. Take for example the many stories in this book. In most of them I have changed the names and sometimes the locations and situations, but they still illustrate the point I'm making to educate you about the action or behaviour I want you to undertake. Let me show you because I didn't think I could tell stories either.

After my epiphany about coaching and how valuable it was to incorporate it into my work, my learning superpower kicked in and I wanted to know all there was about coaching. You might not know it, but coaches speak professionally and professional speakers coach. The two disciplines go hand in hand. So I enrolled in a professional speaking workshop. The facilitator started the event by telling her own story, which had its fair share of personal hardship and tragedy. She ended with, 'Now you're all going to tell your stories!' What the hell? There is nothing interesting in my story and my introvert self was freaking out. I was very uncomfortable to say the least. I don't know what I'd been expecting because for goodness sake, I was at a professional speaking workshop! Long story short, I discovered there was interesting stuff in my story and that I have heaps of stories to tell. All I needed to do was take the time to find them.

There is no way you've spent however long working with your clients to not have stories. Like me, you just need to take the time to find them. I now feel obligated to share my stories because they help people. I help people; it's my why. I never try to explain anything these days without a story. It is the single most effective way to explain something. Try it!

You need to be understood by your clients and people have always learned through the ancient art of storytelling. It just makes sense to incorporate storytelling into your every day. If you've heard me speak, been to one of my workshops, or worked with me, you know I tell stories all the time. Stories make it easier for your audience and clients to learn and accept what you're saying.

Use storytelling to help your client understand and learn.

Active Listening

I've been rabbiting on and saying that changing conversations and building strong relationships with clients is all about asking questions. In Chapter 3 Time to DISCOVER, I gave you three key questions: 'What else?' 'If you did know, what would it be?' and 'How does that make you feel?' I did this so you had go-to questions at hand at all times. You didn't need to think ahead, and this allowed you to listen. It's also the reason I've scripted all the important conversations for you and given you meeting agendas to follow as well. You will do your best work when you have structure around you and will relax into building authentic relationships with clients through active listening and asking questions.

Active listening is a skill that can be acquired and developed with practice. However, it can be difficult to master and it will take time and patience to develop. Active listening means you're fully concentrating on what's being said, rather than just passively hearing what the other person is saying. It involves listening with all your senses and giving full attention to whomever is speaking. It's also important that the active listener is seen to be listening, or the speaker may deduce that they're talking to someone who is not interested. You do this by using both verbal and nonverbal cues like maintaining eye contact, nodding your head, saying yes, hmmm, etc.

I've completed some hypnosis training and as you can imagine, a high level of trust between practitioner and client needs to be built very quickly in order for that modality to be successful. In hypnosis, we were taught mirroring techniques to help build trust quickly: breathing in and out in time with the client, blinking when they blink, mirroring their posture and body language, and maintaining eye contact are all ways to use mirroring.

Active listeners ask open-ended questions like, 'What else?' If you did know, what would it be?' and 'How does that make you feel?' With active listening there can often be pauses in the conversation and short periods of silence, which should be accepted. Just as we need silence to think and to process, sometimes our clients do too. There's no need to jump in and interrupt to fill the void. Just politely wait and listen.

A coach helps people move from where they are now to where they want to be.

You cannot know where someone is right now with their business unless you've asked some great questions and actively listened to the answers. It's impossible for you to know how to help your client move forward without asking and listening in the first place.

Active listening is all about gathering information. It's the perfect medium to quench your thirst for information, allowing your No. 1 Superpower free rein. It involves giving clients time to explore their thoughts and feelings, so take the time needed. Forget about the industry conditioning that says listening to people is a waste of time and unproductive. By not listening to clients, it's come back to bite us. You'll never roll out advisory services without listening. Listening to someone is never a waste of time.

To be effective, you need your clients to listen to you, but to listen to you, you need to listen to them first. Practise using active listening techniques and start building strong and resilient client relationships.

Practise

Practise, practise, practise. Don't fool yourself into thinking you can do this without practice. I know you'll try, and probably more than once. You're extremely time conscious so you'll think, hang it, I'll wing it. I guarantee you won't get a great result if you take this approach. How do I know? Because I did this too! Role-play with a team member or a friend. Put in the time and you'll get a great result.

Living at Cause

One of the greatest life lessons I have learned to date is responsibility for self. Responsibility for yourself, your actions, your words, your thoughts, everything. Until very recently, that's how I referred to it. As mentioned, I've done some training in hypnosis and my teacher and coach spoke about Cause and Effect and Living at Cause.

CAUSE AND EFFECT

C > E

Results   vs   Reasons

Figure 6.2: Cause and Effect

Living at cause means that not only do you take responsibility for the effect you may have on a situation and/or the people and things around you, but you take it one step further and look for a way to positively influence the situation, even if that situation is pretty ugly. I have always believed that anything can be done or framed in a positive mindset. I don't mean you need to be happy all the time, laughing and joking about everything. It's not that, because there is plenty of rubbish that life can throw at you. However, you can always take a realistic approach to things, look at the outcomes, and gain a positive perspective even if it's only a small slither of positivity.

I've talked a little about my family. This attitude to life comes very much from my mother and her side of the family. Nanny, my mum's mum, was always a very positive lady. I remember a time in our family when my mother was quite ill. Diagnosed with bowel cancer, she underwent extensive surgery and then a six-month course of chemotherapy. Things weren't so good but she told us that she was happy it was bowel cancer out of all the other awful cancer-related illnesses because she had heard and believed it was the one that was most easily cured. That's a pretty extreme example but there can be just a glimmer of positivity in anything. That was 15 years ago, and I can report my mum remains cancer-free.

Looking at the Cause and Effect illustration in the figure 6.2 Cause and Effect above, you see it shows that Cause is greater than Effect and that the direction of the arrow points towards Cause. When you are at Effect, you look for reasons things happen, not to improve or learn but to lay blame on anything and everyone that is not you. When you are at Cause, you look for a result, how you influenced the situation, and what you can do to either rectify it or learn and improve for next time. You look for the internal cause, you. You cannot control others, their actions or behaviours, but you can control yours. Here are a few examples of the difference.

Situation	Living at CAUSE	Living at EFFECT
You were late for a meeting	I should have left earlier	The traffic was bad
You didn't go to the gym this week	I need to look at my schedule and plan better	There is so much work to do I can't do everything
You lodged client tax returns late	I will try a different way to get the work in earlier	The client didn't bring the work in early enough
Your team missed a deadline	I'll talk to the team and see how we can better manage deadlines	The team let me down
Clients questioned your bill	It might be time to consider upfront pricing	Clients just don't understand the value
Clients aren't taking up advisory services	I need to find a way to change this	My clients aren't the right type for advisory anyway

Living at Cause

Use the power of your mind and don't forget that you can positively influence ANY situation, good, bad, or ugly.

Living at cause and being a positive influence are the main takeaways from the workshops I run in Authentic Leadership.

Personal growth is an ongoing process of understanding and developing yourself in order to achieve your full potential. It's never over. There is always something to learn. Personal development is a vital part of your personal growth, maturity, success, and happiness. It is the foundation of emotional, physical, intellectual, and spiritual wellbeing. Use living at cause as your compass and never stop looking for ways to positively influence people and situations.

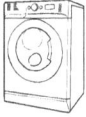

The Real Accountant

Never stop learning and growing as a person. It's key to your success and happiness. Embrace the Real Accountant.

Questions and Red Flags

'I Don't Know any Stories'

You'll have found this chapter a little bit different from the previous process-dominated chapters. Its content is something you would not normally see in an accounting book. After reading it, I'm fairly certain you'll have quite a few questions going through your mind, and red flags popping up such as, 'I don't know any stories.'

Yes, you do, you just need to actively seek them out. Once you focus on something, you'll be surprised at what the universe or to be more specific, your brain, delivers you. Heard of your *reticular* activating *system (RAS)? It's the part of the brain that* helps you see what you would like to see and in doing this, influences your actions. As an example, when you buy a new car, let's say it's a BMW, you'll start to notice BMWs everywhere on the road due to your RAS firing. In the same way, when you start focusing on storytelling, everywhere around you opportunities for stories will arise.

'Why Do I Need to Change Anything?'

'I already actively listen and ask questions of my clients. Why would I need to change anything?'

Think about if you are really actively listening or just planning what to say next. You will have read the information around multi-tasking and how it is completely ineffective. The flipside of multi-tasking is single tasking. It's not only doing one thing at a time, but thinking of one thing at a time. Your No. 4 Superpower, Processing Power, makes it possible for you to solve complex issues in your head. However, it also makes you susceptible to being one step ahead of everyone else, thinking what to say or do next rather than actively and mindfully listening to your clients. Just double check on whether you are actively listening.

Do you interrupt others during a conversation? Forget people's names as soon as you have met them? Finish people's sentences? Check your email while talking on the phone? Fake attention while people are talking? If you do any of these things regularly, you are not practising active listening. It's a skill worth gold when it comes to changing your conversations and delivering advisory services. Work on mastering it.

'This is Tax and Accounting'

'How can I live at cause all the time and be positive? This is tax and accounting, for goodness sake.'

Yes, it is tax and accounting, and it's also much more than that. Remember: you have the power to change people's lives. If you want opportunities to do that, you need to live at cause and be positive. The opportunities simply won't come your way otherwise.

There is always a positive way for you to influence any situation. Just give it go. I guarantee you'll be better for it.

Coming Up

Okey dokey, ready for some more implementation? Let's find out what Leading Edge Business™ is all about.

Actions to Take After Reading This Chapter

1. Write down three client stories you could use to explain a great outcome to other clients.

2. Check out these books:

    a. *Just Listen* by Mark Goulston

    b. *Stories for Work* by Gabrielle Dolan

    c. *The Introvert's Edge* by Matthew Pollard.

3. Draw the Cause & Effect diagram from Figure 6.2 and hang it on your wall where you can see it.

7

Leading Edge Business™

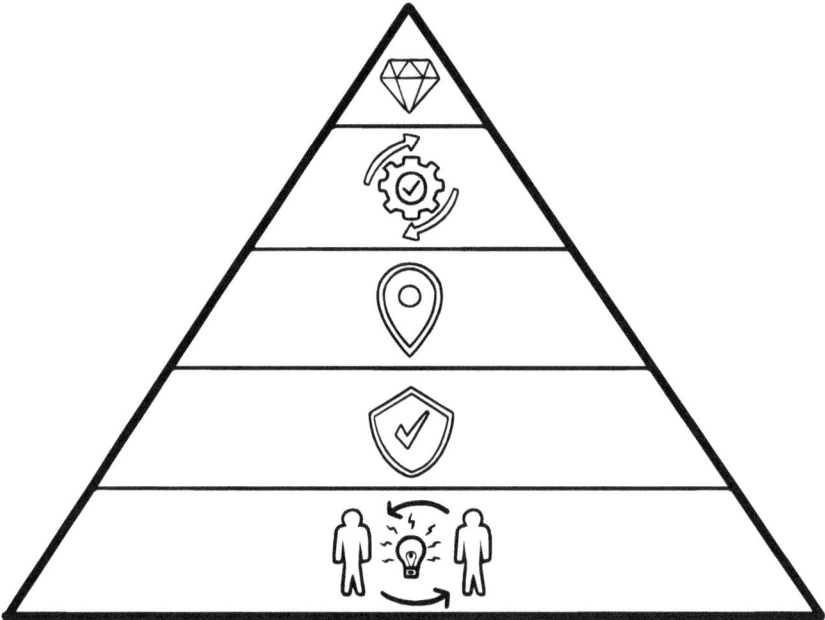

If you can't describe what you are doing as a process, you don't know what you're doing

— W. Edwards Deming[15]

---

15 Goodreads.com, 2019

The perception that delivering advisory services is difficult, unstructured, and complicated is widely held throughout the accounting industry. You're about to learn differently.

Leading Edge Business™ is phase two of The Small Business Project. It is a business advisory delivery model and it encompasses what I call the '5Ps': PLAN, PROTECT, POSITION, PROGRESS, and POWER. Just like Maslow's hierarchy of needs, fulfilling each level in order by starting at the bottom and working upwards ensures sustainable success of the model as a whole.

Leading Edge Business™ is simple and structured. It's designed to effortlessly change your conversations to being forward-focused so you can conduct flawless business advisory meetings. It naturally supports your superpowers and doesn't try to make you into something you're not. It's not about sales, but a straightforward approach for both you and your client to follow as you work together to deliver the future your client wants and dreams of.

Leading Edge Business™ helps you take your client to the next level, consolidating on the Business Metamorphosis® process. It links seamlessly with the 3Ds of Business Metamorphosis®. My unique 5Ps methodology keeps you steady, supported, and focused as you deliver your Leading Edge Business™ services.

It takes more than a good idea or being good at what you do to be successful in business. Leading Edge Business™ enables you to skilfully walk your client through the next steps, moving from their now to their future in an easy, visual, step-by-step process with a clear beginning and end.

Flexible and adaptable, Leading Edge Business™ can be used to deliver all your accounting and business advisory services. You can even build compliance delivery into it if you want to. A Mindshop global business advisory survey found the number one capability required to successfully deliver business advisory services was to have a clear business advisory model (Mindshop, 2019).

Begin with the end in mind   *— Stephen Covey*[16]

Persistently trying to deliver advisory services the old way – looking in the rear-view mirror, where clients cannot see a beginning or an end or even understand why they should be taking up the services – will continue to fail. Clients will only ever engage with advisory services on an ad hoc basis at best, ensuring you and your business remain firmly stuck in the vicious reliance on compliance cycle. Growing your business or even just maintaining your turnover levels will become more and more difficult through the natural attrition of clients and with your continuing reliance on compliance. Pricing pressure on compliance services will continue to increase as technology and artificial intelligence make further in-roads, rendering doing business increasingly difficult and putting you in a regrettable but avoidable position.

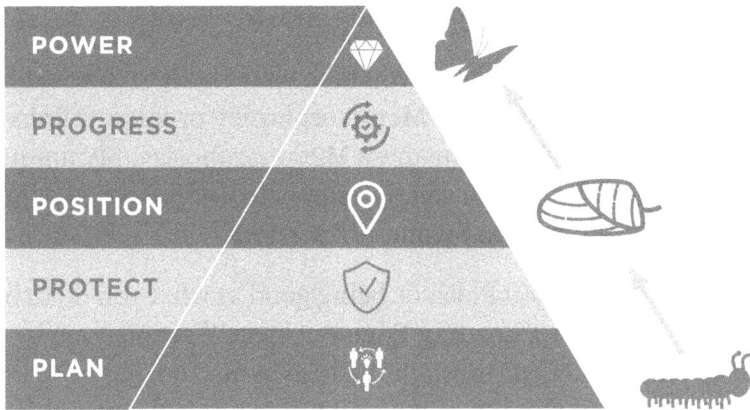

Figure 7.1 The 5Ps

16 Covey, n.d.

The 5Ps

P1: PLAN

PLAN is all about helping your clients capture and formulate the strategic foundation. It is new to the accounting industry and a process that you will not have done before.

You will be aware of the plethora of content, advice, knowledge, and research that confirms the best place (and really only place if you want to succeed) to start in business is with strategy and a strategic foundation. However, due to your detailed operational nature and rear-view focus, you're inclined to dismiss it. Most accountants don't have their own strategic foundation in place, let alone know how to assist their clients with this discipline. This results in the vast majority of small businesses never having a strategic plan or setting strategic goals, just floating along doing what they do, hoping for success but prone to high failure rates. PLAN rectifies the lack of strategic advice and foundation for small businesses.

P2: PROTECT

Almost always when someone in the financial industry refers to protect or protecting, they usually mean some type of insurance. Not so in Leading Edge Business™. The objective of PROTECT is twofold:

1. To ensure your data is clean and correct in order to deliver the right answers

2. To educate your client as a business owner, teaching them what numbers to look at and how to interpret them.

Do this and it's a solid protective foundation for any business and business owner. By arming yourself with information as you collectively protect your client's business, you are enabling informed business decisions. Who wouldn't want that?

P3: POSITION

I don't know about you but I get tired of seeing so much digital advertising on social media platforms promising to build seven-figure businesses overnight with no work or effort on your part. 'Take your business to No.1 in 30 days', and other embarrassing and unrealistic statements promising business success.

It's my belief, as I am certain it will also be yours, that there's no magic pill, no magic wand to wave for business success. Look at any overnight business success story and you'll find it took 10 years in the making. However, if you systematically and diligently plan and work towards having your business in a position ready for growth and expansion, then you have the best chance of success to grow and succeed. Am I right? POSITION is the stage of positioning your client's business ready for growth and expansion. If business owners fail to understand the implications of growth and ignore the need to prepare for it, ignorantly or not, they might just have no business to grow. I don't know about you, but I saw this happen repeatedly when I was practising. At the time, I had nothing in my toolbox to even attempt to prevent it. It was very frustrating. I am giving you the tools. Make good use of them.

P4: PROGRESS

I call this the 'Nike P' because of that brand's famous tagline, 'Just do it.' PROGRESS is simply about getting on with it. You've assisted your client to PLAN, PROTECT, and POSITION. The foundation is complete. It's now time to help your client launch into growth and expansion. You do this by supporting, guiding, analysing, reporting, monitoring, keeping them accountable ... whatever they might need in an advisory capacity to keep them moving forward towards their future.

P5: POWER

The metamorphosis is complete. This is the butterfly stage where your client takes the power back over their business. No longer are they at the beck and call of their business. They are in control.

POWER is about looking to the future and seeing what's possible. It's future-proofing and bringing about some bold plans that your clients might have only ever dreamed about being in a position to undertake. POWER is the final P but it's not the end. To bring to fruition any new initiatives, future-proofing, or next-level ideas formulated in the POWER stage, loop right back around to the first P, PLAN, and start the Leading Edge Business™ process again.

The 5Ps are discussed in detail in the next three chapters.

There are no set or recommended timeframes for working with a client in any one single P of the 5Ps. What a client wants and needs will all depend on them, where their business is at now, what they want to achieve, how fast they want to grow or improve or both, and what their capacity is to fund those changes. You and your client may spend any amount of time working within each of the 5Ps. Each client will most likely be slightly different. I guarantee as you continue to use Leading Edge Business™ with your clients you will start to see patterns of time and effort within each of the 5Ps. This will give you greater power and knowledge to help set your clients' expectations right from the get-go.

The 5Ps are also flexible enough that you may very well find yourself working with your client across two (rarely, sometimes three) levels. I see this happen regularly with P2: PROTECT and P3: POSITION, as these levels often go hand in hand.

Yes, Leading Edge Business™ is a business advisory delivery model that's designed to work from the bottom to the top in a vertical fashion, but life and therefore business don't always work that way. You can easily loop around, move up and down with the 5Ps, without losing the powerful structure and flow that the infrastructure of the model provides. Take for instance a situation for your client like changing market conditions, a legislation change, or a divorce. These may not allow you to proceed forward as you thought, but you don't want your client to feel that they have stalled, are unable to move to the next step, or think they have to stop the advisory program.

Leading Edge Business™ overcomes this. You simply talk to them about consolidating a level or revisiting and revising a lower level, enabling them to be ready to rebuild when things change, and allowing you to continue to deliver consistent advisory services. The services you provide may be in some reduced capacity depending on the severity of the situation, but they will nonetheless be consistent. Leading Edge Business™ is life-and-business-curveball approved!

When to Introduce Leading Edge Business™

When should you introduce Leading Edge Business™ to your clients?

In Chapter 4 DIG, you skimmed over the Leading Edge Business™ model. This let them know that you had their future well in hand, and had plenty to work on with them going forward if they chose to follow that path with you. At the end of the DIG session, your clients would have been overloaded with information, so you needed to be extremely careful not to overwhelm them.

The best time to have a more in-depth conversation about Leading Edge Business™ is when the clients ask for it. After the DIG session, your client would have chosen to proceed in one of five ways:

1. Accepted and agreed to commence the Good package from your proposal

2. Accepted and agreed to commence the Better package from your proposal

3. Accepted and agreed to commence the Best package from your proposal

4. Advised they will undertake and carry out the DIG actions under their own steam

5. Did nothing.

Options 1 to 3 are the triggers to schedule a Leading Edge Business™ meeting with your clients to discuss how you will proceed with their package.

Option 4 is the trigger to set follow-up accountability phone calls for a fortnight and then a month after their DIG session, or when you last spoke to them given you would have touched base in the DELIVER phase to find out how they were travelling with the actions. These clients may not have agreed to a package but through the follow-up process, you may find you have an opportunity to deliver some one-off Leading Edge Business™ solutions regardless.

Clients taking option 4 may be concerned with the time and costs involved in completing Leading Edge Business™ and doubt their ability to complete it successfully. Ask them directly if these are their concerns and work with them to adjust the timing, pricing, and services in the proposal accordingly. Perhaps they just might like to meet with you once a month for accountability purposes and to discuss how they are going. If they still wish to proceed on their own, just let them know you and your team are there to support them. Touch base with them on an informal but regular schedule just to see how they are going.

Option 5, doing nothing, may mean your clients might simply be a little overwhelmed. Bear in mind they would not have worked through DISCOVER, DIG, and DELIVER with you unless they were interested in more advice. They might just need some time and gentle input from you to work out what they need. If you've not heard from them at all during the follow-up phase of DELIVER, then I'd recommend setting at least one more follow-up phone call for 4–6 weeks after the DELIVER follow-up schedule is complete. You will continue to work and be in contact with these clients in a compliance capacity. Use these touch compliance points to touch base with them about Leading Edge Business™.

Scheduling a Leading Edge Business™ meeting with clients is as easy as having your admin team book it, letting the client know you want to discuss the ins and outs of the next steps and what that means for them. The best way to describe the format of the Leading Edge Business™ meeting is that it is similar to a teeny-tiny DIG session.

Here's what you need to do.

Before the Meeting

Revisit the Gaps

Look at the Business Metamorphosis® interactive model that your client completed. Look at where they are now versus where they want to be in the future. Are they a caterpillar wanting to be a chrysalis or a chrysalis wanting to be a butterfly?

Review the client's DISCOVER business score out of 10. Are they a five out of 10, a seven out of 10, or even a nine out of 10? What does their 10 out of 10 look like?

Revise the client's DIG, now, and future comparisons, allowing you to understand and be fully aware of the gaps that you will be assisting the client to bridge.

Sketch out a Leading Edge Business™ Package

Notice the use of the words 'sketch out' as in rough draft or idea, not a detailed, comprehensive, and complete package mapped out to within an inch of your life full of minute details ... keep that No.1 Superpower in check. Here is not where you need it, okay?

You only need to sketch out the next six months at the most. Twelve months is way too long and the client may feel trapped into accepting a long program. Six months is a good dip-your-toe-in-the-water type trial for your client and a timeframe and costing level they will be willing to invest in.

Make sure when you're drafting the Leading Edge Business™ package that you use the 5Ps to structure it. It will be very unlikely that you would be able to deliver the client from P1: PLAN to P5: POWER in six months. I wouldn't even try. For the first six months, focus only on the first three Ps: PLAN, PROTECT, and POSITION.

Bridge the Gaps

Plan how you're going to show your client the Leading Edge Business™ package you've put together which bridges the gaps and moves them towards their desired future. Make sure you're prepared to discuss this.

Speaking Aloud

Make sure you speak aloud when you practise. Don't just think about what you would say by running through it in your mind. While internal monologue is the accountant's go-to technique (we love to do things in our heads), it won't work for practising what to say. As an introvert, you'll struggle to produce the words when you need them if all you've done is think them through. The cat, the dog, or even the chair works well to practise on.

At the Meeting

At the meeting, deliver the same topics in the same order as the 'Before the Meeting' preparation. Start with Revisit the Gaps, follow this by sketching out the Leading Edge Business™ package you've put together, and then bridge the gaps. There is just one extra step to add at the meeting and that's the next steps.

When revisiting the gaps at the meeting, remember:

Focus on the Why

Every meeting starts by revisiting:

1. Your client's Business Metamorphosis® gap, from caterpillar to butterfly

2. Your client's DISCOVER gap, e.g. 'You were a five. We're working towards a 10'

3. Your client's PLAN strategic foundation, their vision, mission, values, and target market.

When sketching out the Leading Edge Business™ package to your clients at the meeting:

Use your Tools

Make sure you have a copy of the Business Metamorphosis® grid model and the Leading Edge Business™ pyramid on hand at all times. They will keep you focused, make you feel safe and secure, and give you the structure you need to have powerful client conversations that deliver consistent and meaningful messages.

At the meeting when discussing how to bridge the gaps, bring to mind:

A coach helps people move from where they are now to where they want to be.

Always refer to you and your client as 'we'. You're a team. There is no 'U' or 'I' in team.

The Next Steps

Until now, you have at no point mentioned the cost of the package. This is by design. You've outlined the package, everything you're going to do, how you're going to deliver it, and discussed how the package bridges the gaps and helps your client move from where they are NOW towards the FUTURE they want.

You wrap up with next steps and it's here that you discuss the cost. Your client has all the information about why they should go through with the Leading Edge Business™ program. You've shown them what it will do for them and the value for their business, so they are now ready to accept a pricing discussion from you. You should not discuss cost any earlier in the process.

It's unlikely that your client will be focused on cost if they have worked through Business Metamorphosis® with you and are now discussing Leading Edge Business™. However, there are always clients whose first question will be, 'What will this cost?' I find the best way to deal with this is to be 100% open and honest and say something like, 'We'll get to talking about cost very shortly. I just need to let you know what's included and how it helps you to move from where you are NOW to where you want to be in the FUTURE. I know it might sound like I'm trying to sidestep the cost question but I'm not. It's just really important to give you all the information you need in the right order. Would that be okay?'

What also happens in next steps is that you book in your PLAN session. Book a date, secure the PLAN session, and go from there. Also let your client know that you will send them a proposal for their acceptance of the upcoming costs and once accepted you can book in the rest of the package meetings. In fact, if you've spent time automating DELIVER and implementing technology, at the end of the meeting you may simply be able to make a couple of proposal changes on the fly and have the client accept the proposal then and there. That's next level and very cool.

Once the proposal has been sent out, you need to follow up. Following up is just as important here as it was in DELIVER. You could use the same follow-up schedule outlined in Chapter 5 Time to DELIVER.

So that's how you go about introducing Leading Edge Business™ and a full Leading Edge Business™ package to your clients.

To wrap up, I want to tell you a story about why I developed Leading Edge Business™ and what makes it so powerful.

I've already spoken about my business consulting journey and my initial struggles with labelling myself as a coach. At the time, I was looking around me and seeing that a lot of business coaching programs were almost always solely focused on sales and marketing. At least, this was my perception at the time. I believed, like many accountants, that coaching was a bit of a taboo subject.

The fact that these programs were not educating their clients about the financial impacts of growth that would be the result of the sales and marketing activities they were advising their clients to undertake distressed me greatly. To me, they were building a house of cards with no strong financial foundation or risk management in place. As finance professionals and accountants, we are aware that if a business owner does not understand the financial impacts of growth, all sales and marketing activities are just a recipe for disaster. Don't get me wrong: sales and marketing are a very important part of business. I have a networking colleague whose tagline is, 'Without sales, business fails,' and he's exactly right. Sales are integral to business, but you need a balanced approach. 'Numbers don't lie', 'the universal language of business', and 'money makes the world go around' – these are clichés for a reason.

That's why as accountants we're so important to the business community. We're the ones with key financial knowledge and the right to provide advice to business owners. We just need to change our conversations to give us the opportunities to showcase and use our knowledge. This is the reason I developed Leading Edge Business™.

The Leading Edge Business™ process when incorporated with Business Metamorphosis® solves one of the biggest problems you as an accountant need to overcome when delivering your services to clients: explaining value.

I want to tell you a little story about Emma. I've known Emma for a long time and first met her when she joined an accounting firm as a trainee accountant where at the time, I was her manager.

Emma is a very accomplished, knowledgeable, young accountant with at least 10 years' experience in accounting and tax. At the time of writing this book, she was a senior client manager. I was having a chat with her one day telling her about everything I was working on and encouraging her to talk to more clients about consulting and advisory work as the next phase and development for her both personally and professionally. Emma let me know that she found advisory services hard to talk about because it seemed so airy-fairy, with no structure or standard outcomes. It made her extremely reluctant and a little scared to raise it with clients.

This was Emma's perception of advisory services. She was and is 100% qualified to talk about advisory services with her clients and would do it with ease. But the fact that she had no structure to rely on to help her know what to talk about, when to talk about it, what questions to ask, or what direction to take the discussion, she felt fearful about even trying to start.

This is why Leading Edge Business™ is so powerful. The 5Ps keep you steady, supported, and focused when you're discussing advisory services. You don't need 20 years of accounting experience before you are able to use it or talk about it. It does not bode well for our industry if it takes more than 10 years of experience before we feel confident enough to talk advisory services with our clients. Since having this conversation with Emma, I have had many more similar conversations with young accounting professionals. They want to help but just don't know how. Leading Edge Business™ along with Business Metamorphosis® is the HOW they can help.

After reading everything in this chapter, you might be asking yourself, 'Why would this business advisory model be any easier to implement than all the others that have come before it? Plenty have failed to make an impact before this.'

That's easy. It was built by me, an introvert and an accountant who has taken the time to gather as much information as I can about what makes accountants tick, where their confidence comes from, and what they are comfortable doing. I used all this knowledge and infused it into Leading Edge Business™.

But of course nothing worth doing is easy. Take your time, gather the information you need, and just make a start.

Just Start

As accountants, we naturally analyse everything and then analyse it again to be sure. There's no 80/20 for us, it's 100% or nothing.

Challenge yourself and just start. It won't be perfect but you'll have started.

As accountants, we like to start with the end in mind. Remember my secret sauce recipe for change? You start with a generous handful of The End Result. Leading Edge Business™ allows you to start this way.

You do this by mapping out your own 5Ps with the list of advisory services you made in Chapter 1 Sex Lies and Revolution. Don't worry, you'll have enough advisory services to fit the model. Just sit back and have a think about it. You're probably giving a lot away for free. Remember: the definition of advisory services in its simplest form is anything that is not compliance.

If you feel you would still like a little more help, I have a special offer for everybody who buys the book. It's called an Advisory Unpack. This is where we step you through unpacking your advisory services and help you slot them into Leading Edge Business™ and the 5Ps. It takes about 45 minutes to work through this with you and you'll have your generous handful of The End Result ready to go. Just turn to the back of the book to claim this offer.

You might still be thinking that you can't offer advisory services, you don't have enough experience, you don't have time, you don't have the team in place, you don't have the right clients ... these are all excuses and you know it. Yes, of course you can. All you need is the structure. No structure makes for very nervous accountants. Remember Emma.

Leading Edge Business™ is all the structure you will need. However, if you would like more information than what's in the book, check out the website https://lyndasteffens.com for the next Leading Edge Business™ three-day workshop where we cover the model and the process and practise the techniques hands-on.

Finally, you might think that this just seems way too simple, too good to be true. How can it be that easy and possibly work? Yes, it is that easy. Remember Superpower No. 4 Processing Power, the ability to process a lot of complex problem-solving in our minds. Because of this and all our other superpowers, we like to O-V-E-R-C-O-M-P-L-I-C-A-T-E things.

Drawing on some more pop culture, which shows you how crazy my love of detail is, I love analysing movies I particularly like. The movie that comes to mind is The Hunger Games: Catching Fire where Beetee in his interview with Caesar Flickerman says if the quarter quell were written into law by men surely it can be unwritten. What on earth does that have to do with accountants and advisory services? you ask. Easy. If we're the ones who have complicated advisory services, then surely we can uncomplicate them and make them easy!

Remember to do the actions at the end of the chapter. Also, keep reading the remaining chapters to learn more about the interpretation of each of the 5Ps and how to roll them out with your clients in a way that works for you and your business.

Actions to Take After Reading This Chapter

1. Download the 5Ps Unpack Template and fill in your advisory services.

2. Check out the Advisory Unpack offer at the back of the book.

You will find the links to download all the documents listed under the above two headings here: https://lyndasteffens.com/bonuses

8

PLAN: The Master Plan

To succeed in business you need a strategy. Without a strategy, businesses lack direction, efficiency, and profitability.

P1: PLAN is the first level and keystone of Leading Edge Business™ and is fundamental to revolutionising how you engage with clients. PLAN is new and different and is the last of the big three implementation chapters.

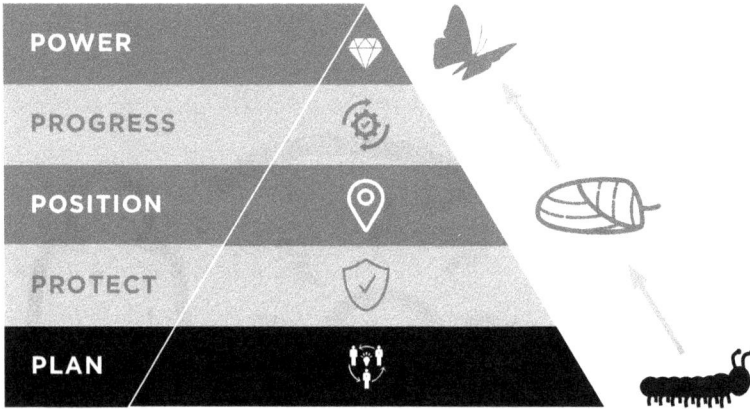

Figure 8.1 The 5Ps and PLAN

This chapter contains a lot of content and yes, it has some feeling stuff in it too.

If you think that strategic advice is hard to deliver, think again.

PLAN makes strategic advice easy. It's all about knowing what questions to ask.

Break the mould, stop focusing on the rear view, and start looking forward. Stand out from the crowd and ensure that your business and your services remain relevant by raising the bar on business advisory services. Plenty of accountants offer strategic advice as a service, but are they really delivering strategic advice? What I do know is that very few if any will be undertaking this type of meeting. PLAN is super-powerful stuff. It will set you above all your competitors and make you stand out as a business advisor who everyone will want to work with.

No longer is strategic advice the domain of management consultants and the like. Collaborate with your clients to set a strategic foundation to build on, providing both you and your client the map for your business advisory journey.

Let your No.1 Superpower off the leash and let it run rampant as you gather all the information you need to understand why your clients do what they do. Get the big picture for what they want to achieve. Satisfy your need for information in turn, making you more confident and comfortable moving forward with business advisory services.

One in five small to medium enterprises (SMEs) would like to receive help from their accountant with their business strategy, on top of the services they already receive.

A goal without a plan is just a wish — Antoine de Saint-Exupery[17]

The Feeling Stuff

Yes, you have to ask the feeling questions. Get used to it.

You'll need some quiet time to sit down and read this chapter so you can take it all in. I don't recommend skim-reading. Get ready for some mind-blowing content.

PLAN is the first P in the 5Ps of Leading Edge Business™. It is the process of building your client's strategic foundation. The strategic foundation of a business encompasses a vision, a mission, the business values, and their target market. BHAG – pronounced 'bee-hag' and meaning 'Big Hairy Audacious Goal' – is a term coined by James Collins and Jerry Porras in their 1994 book *Built to Last*. A BHAG is a goal that is highly emotive. It may be externally questionable but it is not regarded as internally impossible. Let me explain what I mean. As an example, my BHAG is to 'reverse global business failure rates'. Others question my goal, so this is what

---

17 Goodreads.com, 2019

externally questionable means. 'Really Lynda, can you accomplish that? It's pretty unrealistic even for you. Is it even possible?' My team and I both believe we can make a positive difference to the global business failure rates. We believe we can achieve the goal, so to us, it is not impossible. This is what not internally impossible means. A BHAG is used to focus a business or organisation on the big picture.

A PLAN meeting takes three to four hours to complete, so you can do it in a morning or an afternoon. At the time of writing this book, I recommend that you price a PLAN meeting at a minimum of $1,650 inclusive of GST. As with pricing a DIG session, if you're working with more than one or two people in the room, you may consider increasing the price. It's much more demanding and requires a greater skill level to facilitate a PLAN meeting with more people present.

For the next section of this chapter, I'll be using my current strategic foundation as an example. See Figure 8.2 below. As with all the implementation chapters, you'll find it easier to follow along if you have a hard copy of the PLAN Detailed Agenda. Go and download a copy of the agenda now: https://lyndasteffens.com/bonuses

Vision	Change lives
Mission	Revolutionise conversations in the accounting industry
Values	Bold Brave Real
Target Market	Motivated accountants, keen to learn and do better
BHAG	Reverse global business failure rates

Figure 8.2 The Small Business Project – Strategic Foundation – 2019

A little scared of doing a strategic advice meeting with your clients? I understand. I was too, but I can wholeheartedly say it's well worth the risk. All you need to do is be prepared, follow the PLAN Detailed

Agenda, and use your Bonus Questions. It's all here for you. I've left nothing out and I've got your back.

Before you jump feet first into PLAN, remember:

Facilitating not Participating

You're asking questions, not providing answers.

You won't know the answers.

A coach stimulates clients' self-discovery by asking powerful questions.

Use your Tools

Make sure you have a copy of the Business Metamorphosis® model and the Leading Edge Business™ pyramid on hand at all times. They will keep you focused, make you feel safe and secure, and give you the structure you need to have powerful client conversations that deliver consistent and meaningful messages.

Out of your Comfort Zone

Yes, this is new, yes, this is different, yes, it is foreign to you, and yes, it will take practice and effort.

Here's how you roll out P1: PLAN.

Before the Meeting

Your PLAN meeting will have been booked either when your Leading Edge Business™ package was accepted or at your Leading Edge Business™ meeting. Prior to the meeting, make sure that your admin team have followed up and confirmed the day, time, and place of the meeting with your clients. Have them reassure the client that they are already fully prepared for the meeting because they are the experts in their business and already know all the answers. You're just going to help them verbalise the answers to get them out. Send your clients the PLAN Client Agenda to give them some idea of what you will discuss at the meeting.

On the day of the meeting, make sure your room is all set up and your whiteboard and notes are prepped and ready to go when the client arrives.

OUR PLAN FOR TODAY
WHEN WHY HOW WHAT WHO

Figure 8.3 Our Plan for Today

To prep the whiteboard, refer to Figure 8.3 above. Write the heading 'Our Plan for Today' and underneath that write 'When, Why, How, What, & Who' in that order. There is no need to write any more than that even though there is more to the diagram. I'll tell you why in just a minute.

As with your DIG session, you will need to have an easel with butchers paper and perhaps some more of those large sticky notes. You will need at least five pieces of butchers paper or five jumbo sticky notes. You prepare these with the following headings:

- 'Why' on the first sheet

- 'How' on the second sheet

- 'What' on the third sheet

- 'Who' on the fourth sheet

- 'Action Plan' on the fifth sheet. The Action Plan sheet has three columns: Action, Due Date, and Responsibility.

Meetings Need Action Plans

In any meeting you're keeping an Action Plan.

Action plans need detail:

a.   What the action is – be clear and concise

b.   When the action is to be completed by

c.   Who is responsible for completing the action.

Ensure that you have your PLAN Detailed Agenda printed and ready on the table, your list of Bonus Questions, Value Words, Business Metamorphosis® and Leading Edge Business™ models, and any other tools ready at hand if you need to refer to them at any time.

Make up kits of laminated materials/resources for your boardroom and meeting rooms so Business Metamorphosis® and the Leading Edge Business™ materials are always handy.

Next, on the whiteboard, write the client's name and business name along with the two Business Metamorphosis® gaps you will revisit: (1) The stage: Caterpillar (C), Chrysalis (Ch) or Butterfly (B), and (2) Their business rating out of 10 from DISCOVER.

For the Business Metamorphosis® stage, note down the one they identified as their NOW which most likely will be Caterpillar (C) or Chrysalis (Ch), and the stage at where they would like to be in the FUTURE. For most business owners this will be Butterfly (B). You'll write this on the whiteboard represented as C or Ch or B with the business rating next to that, say 5/10. These will help to prompt you and keep you on track when you're opening the meeting.

This all sounds like a lot of effort. Why do you need to be so prepared?

Because accountants are so time conscious from a compliance perspective, we sometimes think we can skip over preparation and just wing it. We've been through it all in our heads, it sounds pretty straightforward, nothing could go wrong, right? Wrong. Our superpowers can trick us and set us up to fail. Just because we think we have it straight in our heads, it does not always play out that way when our clients are in front of us and we're in the middle of a meeting. This is one of the challenges of being an introvert.

With meetings like these that are not necessarily familiar to you, preparation gives you structure and keeps you on track and focused. That's why you prepare the whiteboard with so much information and you have all your tools around you to prompt you all the way through the meeting. They are pieces of information you can draw on if you happen to get stuck.

This preparation addresses the real concern around not being able to answer client questions, or of meetings stalling and not knowing what to say. As an introvert, you need these prompts and materials around you. Don't let your superpowers trick you into failing.

Don't Set Yourself up to Fail

Give yourself plenty of time, be prepared, gather information, follow the system, practise and pick an easy target – that is, don't start with the most difficult client on your books.

During the Meeting

Your client has arrived and you're about to start the meeting. The overall objective of a PLAN meeting is to finish with a fully formed strategic foundation for your client, but this may not always be possible, so don't be put off if it doesn't happen. What you will have achieved is the start of your client's strategic foundation and a guide for moving forward for both you and the client. If this is the case and you finish the meeting without a fully formed strategic foundation, you may wish to spend a little time in future monthly meetings tidying it up and refining it until you are happy. Remember: strategic foundations are not set in stone. They are fluid and they move with the business. Particularly in the first three to five years of business, they are very likely to change and sometimes dramatically every 12 months or so, so do not spend a lot of time trying to get the first strategic foundation for your client fully formed.

You can see from the PLAN Detailed Agenda there are 10 steps for a successful PLAN meeting. Just be prepared for this meeting to jump around a little bit. The first four steps and the last two steps, 9 and 10, stay firmly in their order of appearance. However, steps 5 through to 8 may need to be quite fluid in how you deliver them. To keep the meeting flowing and to help your client verbalise all the things they need to get out for strategic foundation, you might need to jump around a little bit and that's okay. The same as strategic and big picture stuff is not always easy for us, neither is it for our clients. Remember that they've probably never really sat down and thought about their business in a big picture strategic sense before, and certainly never has anyone bothered to ask them any questions about it. The fact you are bothering to do so makes you a powerhouse of strategic knowledge for them.

As you work through the flexible steps 5 through 8, I'll fill you in on more details about how to keep the meeting flowing, why you might want to jump around, and which steps are the easiest to jump to. I've got your back, remember!

Oh, and don't sit down. Your clients can obviously sit down during the meeting, but you need to be up on your feet, moving about, writing notes, staying in control, and keeping the meeting flowing.

The 10-Step PLAN

Step 1 – Revisit Gaps, Set Expectations, Why we Build a Strategic Foundation

Every meeting in The Small Business Project starts with the why. PLAN is no different. A quick refresh of this all-important information gets the meeting off to a great start. No, you cannot skip this part. If you do, the meeting will not be as effective as it should be. Follow the system, okay? Even if you met with the client the day before, you still start your PLAN meeting by taking another look at the why.

Don't Set Yourself up to Fail

Give yourself plenty of time, be prepared, gather information, follow the system, practise, and pick an easy target – that is, don't start with the most difficult client on your books.

Revisiting the gaps is easy. The prompts are already on the whiteboard for you. Start with Business Metamorphosis® and the gap in the stages your client initially identified between their NOW and their FUTURE. Move quickly across to the business rating score from DISCOVER. The purpose of revisiting the gaps is to evoke all the same emotions your client felt during their DISCOVER session, which can be quite emotional when they first looked at Business Metamorphosis®. Remember: business is emotional and it's crucial you use these emotional hooks to set every meeting off on the right foot. Remind your client that you're here today to work together to build their business from a caterpillar to a butterfly and an x out of 10 to a 10 out of 10. Remind them that being an x out of 10 doesn't feel very good and if they were to stay that way they said it would feel … Use a couple of the bad words you gathered in DISCOVER. Then move into why you build a strategic foundation. Use the content at the beginning of this chapter to explain to your client why you insist on building a strategic foundation and the reason it is the key foundational step of Leading Edge Business™ – without strategy, businesses lack direction, efficiency, and therefore profitability.

Strategic foundations help keep everybody on track with big picture goals, enabling business owners to empower their employees and their team so that they can share in the decision-making. Provided that decisions are made in line with the business' strategic foundation, then for the most part, the owners and directors will be happy with those decisions. A strategic foundation is a vital part of leveraging and scaling a business. You cannot grow a business on your own, you need other people, and involving other people in your business without having direction and a plan for the future is just asking for trouble. Without a strategic foundation you will be stuck working in the business rather than on the business because everyone in the team will simply look to the business owner for all the answers, resulting in no initiative being taken, no innovation being created, and no growth being generated. And just think about the efficiency of a business where the business owner needs to answer and direct every little decision or task. There are only so many hours in a day and a person can only be in so many places at once. It's simply inefficient, tiring, and unsustainable.

A strategic foundation goes a long way to avoiding these problems. It also makes your job as their advisor guiding their business journey much easier and efficient. You know where they want to go and why they want to go there. It's extremely powerful stuff. I wasn't going to explain the importance of a strategic foundation in detail because you can find it all on Google, but hey, I can't seem to stop and I hope you feel my passion coming through loud and clear as to why this is so important.

A strategic foundation is also fundamental to the formulation of your client's business messages and will assist your client with their marketing efforts. When clients work through the PLAN process, they become extremely clear around their why. They are ready to go out and conquer the world. Just you wait. By the end of your first PLAN meeting, the energy that you create in the room is intoxicating and you'll want to do more and more and more. Ooh, it's exciting. Simon Sinek said, 'People don't buy what you do they buy why you do it.'

Adding to this burgeoning list of why every business needs a strategic foundation is that it makes accountability very easy to roll out, both for the business owner and for you as their advisor. Accountability is a key part to delivering the business future that your client will want.

Accountability is the most powerful of coaching methodologies.

Step 2 – Our Plan for Today

Our Plan for Today is a visual representation of the meeting agenda and it provides the key steps and their order for your PLAN meeting. We love words and information (Superpower No. 1) but our clients not so much, so presenting this visually is much more appealing and engaging for them. It also keeps the energy in the room on a high. This is why you only prepped the whiteboard with the heading. It's now time to complete the rest of the diagram for your clients. I've made a little video for you to download so that you can see me draw and present Our Plan for Today, including how I explain it to clients. Although making a video is pretty hard for me, 20-plus takes being my average (I'd never make it as an actress), it's much easier for me to do a three-minute video than it is to write three pages in this book.

Go and check out the video now to see how it's done. You can access it here: https://lyndasteffens.com It's very simple and easy but don't underestimate it. You need to practise and perfect it before holding your first PLAN meeting.

Speaking Aloud

Make sure you speak aloud when you practise. Don't just think about what you would say by running through it in your mind. While internal monologue is the accountant's go-to technique (we love to do things in our heads), it won't work for practising what to say. As an introvert, you'll struggle to produce the words when you need them if all you've done is think them through. The cat, the dog, or even the chair works well to practise on.

Don't think that you can draw the whole diagram on the whiteboard before the meeting. It doesn't work and the explanation will be ineffective.

Drawing the diagram on the whiteboard with your clients in the room adds a little theatre to the meeting. It also gets you out of your seat, showcases you as an advisor, shows that you have control of the meeting, and gives the meeting structure. It puts you in a power position, and settles your nerves because this little two-minute intro will be something you've practised over and over and over again. You'll be able to deliver flawlessly and frankly, it looks good.

Remember I said that you would be on your feet for the whole meeting? Well, if you happen to need a little break and would like to sit down for five minutes – because sometimes, standing on your feet for three hours can be quite demanding, especially in heels (I don't recommend it, fellas), then have your client stand up and take the notes. You will need to direct them, telling them what to write, but it will get them up and moving and can create a different energy in the room. Killing two birds with one stone by having your client take the notes helps with meeting engagement and flow as well as giving you a little rest.

Movement creates energy, so position your easel and sticky notes around the room so you have to move around to use them, changing where you're standing and speaking from.

No more boring meetings where you just sit at the boardroom table and look at each other. Boring meetings is not what PLAN is about and certainly not what The Small Business Project is all about. Engaged and energetic meetings is where it's at!

Step 3 – WHEN

This is the part of the PLAN meeting where you start to formulate your client's strategic foundation. Let's start this section of the meeting with the easiest part. WHEN is quick, it's easy, and you can just get it out of the way. You touched on strategic advice in DIG because strategic advice is all about looking forward to the future, and the easiest way to measure the future is by the number of years. Generally, in strategic advice when we talk about the future we mean 10 years. It's far enough away to be the future but close enough that our human heads can still envisage what it might look like. Trying to go any further out, things get fuzzy. We don't want that, and it's easy to work out: if it's 2019 now, your WHEN is 2029.

Now, remember in DIG I told you to look out and check for future milestones? In most cases they won't impact the WHEN of 10 years unless those milestones are winding up the business or retirement. There would be no point developing a business' strategic foundation for 10 years if your client intends to sell the business to fund their retirement in five years. For major milestones that radically change the business operations, use the shorter milestone instead of 10 years.

Step 4 – BHAG

Big Hairy Audacious Goal. I love this term. It's so out there for accountants. Your clients will be blown away that you're even using a term like this because up until now, you've probably been so straighty-one-eighty with them. If you are a bit shy to use the term at first, you can just call it 'your big future goal' but go on, take a chance. Oh no, another song, *Take a Chance on Me* by Abba, a lovely tune to have buzzing about in your head for a couple of hours. Sorry not sorry.

Right, back to being serious, let's look at the definition of a BHAG again: a goal that is highly emotive, maybe externally questionable, but not regarded as internally impossible. It's pretty out there. A BHAG will lead you directly to why people do what they do. You will need to push yourself and your client in this step to get them out of their comfort zone and into the big picture. For them to say their BHAG is to earn a million dollars, while it's a place to start if that's all you can get, it's not emotive enough.

By way of example, take a look at my BHAG 'reverse global business failure rates'. Turn back a few pages to Figure 8.2 to find it. It has the characteristics of being highly emotive, and it's 100% externally questionable but regarded as internally possible. Is it a realistic goal? Can it actually be achieved? I absolutely believe that I can reverse global business failure rates through coaching and educating accountants to change their conversations, and my team does as well. This BHAG unites us.

The easiest way to get your client to think big is to ask some great questions. Guess what? I've put together a list of PLAN Bonus Questions for you. Download them here: https://lyndasteffens.com Over time, you'll add your own to the list but this will get you started.

A coach stimulates clients' self-discovery by asking powerful questions.

Check out the PLAN Bonus Questions and start practising facilitating clients' BHAGs. If you're asking questions, don't forget to TAKE NOTES. Jot down the key words and phrases your client uses. You'll instinctively know the most powerful ones when they come along, so use these to dig further. Don't worry about what words to write down. Write them all down to start with. The more PLAN meetings you do, the better you will get at notetaking. It's much better to have pages of notes to work with than nothing at all.

Step 5 – WHY (Vision)

You can see how talking about a client's BHAG directly leads you to their WHY. It's a natural extension. The BHAG is what they will do and the WHY is why they do it, of course.

I'm reversing global business failure rates because I want to change lives. Refer to Figure 8.2.

Let me tell you why I chose to work with the accounting industry rather than setting up my own business coaching empire. Simple. If I can help accountants change their lives and businesses, then by extension they will help hundreds of small business owners way more than I could possibly help these businesses through business coaching. The reach is greater and it's never been about me. It's about you. I believe in you, guys, I love accountants.

The PLAN Bonus Questions you used in the previous step work just as well for Step 5. Use your PLAN Bonus Questions and start probing around your client's WHY. Getting big picture and strategic can be challenging at the best of times for our clients, so it might take a bit of work to get the WHY. Here's where the fluidity of steps 5 through 8 come in very handy. You can always come back to the WHY and in most PLAN meetings that's what I do. WHY is the last thing we pull together.

Just keep poking and prodding, asking a lot of questions, and you'll get what you need. Remember to TAKE NOTES. I can't say this enough. It's too easy to get caught up in the energy of the meeting and forget the job you're doing. Again, with practice you'll get more adept at notetaking. Just write down everything to begin with. Better to have pages of notes to work with than nothing at all. Perhaps if you find it really difficult you could have one of your admin team sit in the meeting to take notes. I'm a big proponent of joint meetings to train your team, so if you want to train another business advisor have them join the meeting where their number one job is to take notes.

Just like in DIG, an easy place to start with finding a client's WHY is by asking about money. How much do you want to earn? What will you do with the money that you earn? What will earning that money do for you and your family? Keep investigating, digging, poking, and prodding because your clients will always have a higher purpose for doing what they do. I have a client whose WHY (vision) is to 'Achieve financial freedom and still be a good bloke, boss, and business owner'. WHYs don't need to be world-changing. They are whatever is appropriate to your client.

When you're forming the vision from your client's WHY, it may be a sentence like my client's above, or a couple of words like mine, or even a list of words. My first vision was just three words 'Learn, Share, Connect'.

Step 6 – HOW (Mission)

HOW is self-explanatory. HOW will you deliver your vision? In my case, HOW will I go about delivering my vision of changing lives? (See Figure 8.2.) Well, you know the answer because you already have my mission, my how: I'll achieve my vision by 'revolutionising conversations in the accounting industry'.

The HOW, mission, or core focus of the business, all these terms are interchangeable but I like to stick to the HOW and the mission as they often have something to do with what your client's business actually does. As you can see, mine is about change, conversations, and the accounting industry. You also already know that I chose to work with accountants to deliver my BHAG and WHY (vision), as the potential reach for changing lives was greater.

The HOW (mission) of another of my business coaching clients who builds websites is to 'build websites that consistently generate leads and sales online'.

To facilitate your client's HOW, start with what their business actually does and work your way out from there.

If at any point you feel like you need to briefly gather your thoughts, here's what you can do.

Gathering your Thoughts

If you need to gather your thoughts, turn to the whiteboard, the butchers paper, or the sticky notes and jot something down. It doesn't need to be anything of great importance. You can just say, 'I don't want to forget that so I'll note it down now.' Meanwhile, you've had 30 seconds or so to gather your thoughts.

One of our challenges as introverts is that we're not fabulous at speaking off the cuff. That's because we process thoughts internally and not externally like extroverts. Extroverts talk and think at the same time. We think then talk. There's also no issue with just saying, 'Give me a minute to think on that.' I often say this. Clients generally think nothing of it and pay little attention. They get very used to how I work.

Step 7 – WHAT (Values)

WHAT your client's core values are, WHAT their business is, and WHAT traits they need to deliver their strategic foundation. Often, we see run-of-the-mill values that a marketing consultant has splayed across a company website: honest, trustworthy, friendly, professional, etc., etc., are some of the terms that come to mind on accounting firm websites. My question is, if you're not already honest, professional, and trustworthy as an accountant, why are you in the industry in the first place? You wouldn't last long without these qualities. For marketing purposes, these values are important but for strategic foundation purposes, you need something a little more challenging and with a bit more oomph. The WHAT is for your client and helps drive them towards achieving their goals. They may or may not use them in marketing. That would be up to the marketing professionals and consultants, which I and most accountants are not. In my case, I do market my WHAT (values) – bold, brave, and real – because they explain how we're going to work together, but not every business' WHAT will be like that.

The purpose of the WHAT is to elicit the values and traits that drive the business internally, how they conduct themselves, how they work together, how they work with their clients, customers, suppliers, and all other stakeholders in the fulfilment of their strategic goals, so they can't be just run-of-the-mill random things.

The best questions to ask in this step are, 'WHAT way will you need to act to deliver your strategic goals (insert whatever you've come up with so far for their BHAG and WHY) that you're not already doing now? What do you need to be better at?'

I had one accounting firm that had just one value: 'resolute'. They were finding that their clients and their team were controlling the business and they were allowing it to happen. As business owners and directors, they were struggling to keep things on track. When I worked with them on their strategic foundation, they realised they needed to set their rules of the game. The value they needed to challenge themselves on every single day was being resolute and sticking to their rules of the game, not letting others direct the flow of traffic.

You might like to Google 'value words'. When I was writing this book, I went back and added a list of value words to your preparation tools for a PLAN meeting, so get Googling. There are plenty of lists available online that will help get your WHAT juices flowing. For that reason I haven't included them as an additional resource. I'll leave that one up to you.

The sweet spot for the number of values for a business is three or five, but you can have any number. A word of warning: more than five and they get a little bit confusing and messy, so I recommend cutting the list down to five or under. As you can see in my previous example, having just one value was super-powerful. Size doesn't matter. Wow, did I just say that!

When you're in WHAT brainstorming mode with your clients, you will probably have a list of 20-plus value-type words. A great way to start narrowing these down is to go back over each one and ask your client how they feel about each one relative to the others.

To narrow down WHAT options, ask your client to pick their top five. Then narrow them down further by looking at similar words in those options. Ask your client to choose the ones that mean the most to them.

I use the voting system when I work with groups. List the WHAT words one by one and ask the group to vote by a show of hands. This makes getting down to a top three or five just that little bit quicker.

Wow, that's Step 7 out of 10 finished. By the time you've got this far, your client will have been working hard and mostly outside of their comfort zone, so they might be a little bit bamboozled and discombobulated. See what I did there? My favourite word again! This is a great time to have a 15-minute break, get up, walk around, stretch your legs, get some tea, coffee, nibbles, have a toilet break, or get some fresh air, whatever it takes.

Step 8 – WHO (Target Market)

WHO is simply your client's target market. WHO do they want as clients and customers, WHO benefits the most from their products or services, WHO sees the most value in what they do? Watch out because almost everyone when asked who their target market is says everyone! That's not true and it's important to get specifics. I do a significant amount of networking and one of my group's core teachings is to be specific about your referral request. Specific is Terrific! We're going to get very specific with your client's WHO.

You need to start with the usual demographic information. For example, one to three partner accounting firms with three or more staff on the Gold Coast in Australia. Quite a number of businesses don't even think about their customers in this light, so even this will be new and ground-breaking for your client.

You have the demographic information, but what are the true characteristics of the people they would like to work with, their character traits? Are they happy, friendly, nice, open to advice, etc., etc. The easiest way to draw this out of your clients is to ask them who they enjoy working with and who they don't, and explain WHY they do or don't enjoy working with them. Both questions are in the PLAN Bonus Question list for you.

You will have noted that my target market is motivated accountants who are keen to learn and do better. That's pretty specific, right?

You're almost there. Just steps 9 and 10 to go.

Earlier in the chapter I mentioned that you might need to be fluid with the order in which you undertake steps 5 through to 8 with your clients, to keep the meeting flowing and to avoid it stalling.

If you're stuck, the easiest step to jump to is Step 8 – WHO. Target markets are the easiest to put together. The second easiest to jump to is Step 7 – WHAT. Values also flow fairly easily.

WARNING: Don't go thinking you can turn steps 7 and 8 into steps 5 and 6 and do them first. You must first attempt steps 5 and 6, the WHY and the HOW, in that order, to get your clients (and you for that matter) thinking big picture. If you don't, and you've already done steps 7 and 8, I guarantee the meeting will stall and you'll have nowhere to go. Keep steps 7 and 8 firmly up your sleeve and only do them out of order if you need to. That's why in the PLAN Detailed Agenda, steps 5 and 6 have been allocated more time than the other steps. They take a bit longer to formulate.

Remember: I said right back at the start of this chapter if the WHY and the HOW don't come out as clean as you would like, you will have plenty to start working with and time to clean them up a little. A strategic foundation is never set in stone.

The more practice you have with PLAN meetings, the better you will become. You will find it easy and almost instinctual to recognise and pluck out the important words to include in your client's strategic foundation.

Out of your Comfort Zone

Yes, this is new, yes, this is different, yes, it is foreign to you, and yes, it will take practice and effort.

Practise

Practise, practise, practise. Don't fool yourself into thinking you can do this without practice. I know you'll try, and probably more than once. You're extremely time conscious so you'll think, hang it, I'll wing it. I guarantee you won't get a great result if you take this approach. How do I know? Because I did this too! Role-play with a team member or a friend. Put in the time and you'll get a great result.

By this time in the meeting you'll be starting to get a very good feel for your client's strategic foundation. It's now time to bring it all together.

Step 9 – Finalise and Educate

In this step, you summarise the strategic foundation and start to pull it all together. Find a fresh piece of notepaper or clean section of the whiteboard and start by writing up each component in this order:

- WHY (vision)

- HOW (mission)

- WHAT (values)

- WHO (target market)

- BHAG.

Your client's WHY, HOW, and BHAG may be a sentence or two each. The WHAT is a list of three to five words, and the WHO will be a few words describing their ideal client.

As you begin to summarise, read it aloud, over and over from top to bottom. This helps with refining all the components as they become one strategic foundation. This is a collaborative effort so ask your client to pitch in and help out.

While I have a great process and formula for developing a strategic foundation for your client, it will not always come out fully formed by the end of your first meeting. I can't reiterate this enough. Some clients find it a little more difficult than others and that's okay. It's not a reflection on you as a strategic advisor or facilitator. What you will ALWAYS achieve with a PLAN meeting is clarity. You and your client will have obtained more insight into their business in the last three hours than you most likely have achieved over a number of years working with them, so do not be put off by not achieving a fully formed strategic foundation. It will happen.

Write up the strategic foundation so it's all together and on one page. Now you need to educate your client on how to use it. Your clients will already be highly engaged with their strategic foundation so they'll be keen to know what to do next. Storytelling works a treat here, and perhaps you could tell the story about using your own strategic foundation, or you can use mine.

Number 1. Your strategic foundation is the go-to for any business decision-making, whether those decisions are big or small. It automates decision-making by reminding your clients of the strategic code they have agreed to keep to for their business. It makes decision-making quick, easy, and consistent. For example, say your client is looking at sponsoring a local footy team and putting their name on the jerseys. They might also be asked to speak at a local business networking function. They are unable to do both activities. Which activity should they do?

Use the strategic foundation to determine if their WHO (target market) is at either of those events. Then look at doing either or both of those events encompassing the values they wish to uphold. Is either of these marketing activities part of their HOW and/or will they bring the client one step closer to delivering their WHY (vision) and their BHAG?

Take me, for example. Using my strategic foundation, speaking at a networking function would put me in touch with the local business community and allow me an opportunity to speak about my BHAG and how I intend to implement my strategic foundation. In so doing, I would be furthering my cause to change lives. The sponsorship of the local footy team's jerseys, albeit a good cause, would not assist with my strategic foundation.

Step your client through one or two examples of how they use their strategic foundation for decision-making to ensure they understand before they leave the meeting.

Number 2. The power of a strategic foundation sits firmly with being able to empower others to make decisions on your behalf, in turn leveraging your time and skills as a business owner. Encourage your client to discuss the strategic foundation with their team, if they have one, so everyone is on the same page taking the initiative, innovating, and growing into their everyday tasks. In fact, if your client has a team, discussing their strategic foundation with the team is an action for them to go away and implement.

Step your client through one or two examples of how to use their strategic foundation to empower others, their team, their spouse, their consultants, you, and whomever else works with them on a consistent basis in the business.

Step 10 – Action Plan and Next Steps

There are always three actions that your client must complete as a result of undertaking a PLAN meeting:

1. Make it visible. Your client needs to make their strategic foundation visible in the office and/or working environment. There are quite a few ways in which they can do that. They may stick it on their wall or the noticeboard, make it the company computer screensaver, have a laminated version typed up and put on their team's desk, or at the water cooler or the coffee machine, in the front of their diaries, or wherever the team regularly looks. It needs to be highly visible.

2. Use it. Start to refer to their strategic foundation for all decision-making, aligning all decisions with it. Step through using it regularly until they form a habit. This is something you can check on in upcoming accountability sessions.

3. Communicate it. Talk to their team, clients, customers, and/or stakeholders. Talking to others makes them accountable. Your clients may also wish to use some of the strategic foundation in their marketing materials. In any case, they just need to start talking about it.

Congratulations! You've reached the end of the meeting and will no doubt have completely tuckered your client out. One of our superpowers is processing a lot of information in our minds but for the most part, it's not like that for our clients. They'll be pretty worn out after the PLAN session, that's why I recommend you give them only three action items to contend with. This will ensure they go away and think about it.

After the Meeting

Right, so your client has left. Have your admin team take photos of all the notes. If you're a neat writer, you could offer the sticky notes to the clients to take away to make the strategic foundation immediately visible. Admin file the notes and diarise any action items or follow-ups you need to make with your client. I recommend touching base with a quick phone call within seven days of your PLAN meeting just to see how they are travelling with their action items. If they have made little progress, encourage them to start. They have invested the time and money to undertake PLAN with you so they should make it count.

Whoa, a huge implementation chapter, are you freaking out? It's all okay, keep calm, keep reading, I'm going to deal with the freak-outs right now.

Freak-out No. 1. You're an accountant, not a strategic advisor. There's no way you can run a meeting like that.

I'll let you in on a secret. Most strategic advisors will not have run a meeting like this either because in my experience, there is not a lot of true strategic advice out there for the taking. You have a full agenda and a full list of Bonus Questions to ask. They will keep the meeting flowing. In addition to that, you've got an instructional video that shows you how to get the meeting started, and everything you need to know about facilitating a PLAN meeting in this chapter. I have 100% faith in my system. I know it works because I use it and I have faith that you will be able to use it too. You've got this! If you do still feel you would like some more help, just go to my website https://lyndasteffens.com and check out when our next Leading Edge Business™ workshop is. PLAN is one of the big implementation areas and we cover it extensively in our three-day workshop.

Freak-out No. 2. I can't pick what I'm having for dinner without getting bogged down in the detail. How on earth am I going to stay big picture enough?

Yes, you are right there, getting and staying big picture can be tricky for us detail-minded people. It will take a little bit of practice. That's why I have built all this structure for you to use – process, scripts, agendas, and Bonus Questions – to ensure you stay on track. And I guarantee even on your first go, you'll provide your client with more clarity and thought-provoking information about their business than anyone has ever done before. They will value every second of your PLAN meeting. They won't need to tell you, you'll feel it, and when you get the confirmation from the energy in the room and your enthusiastic clients who want to work with you more and more, you'll want to do more and more and simply be better at it. The trick is starting.

Just Start

As accountants, we naturally analyse everything and then analyse it again to be sure. There's no 80/20 for us, it's 100% or nothing.

Challenge yourself and just start. It won't be perfect but you'll have started.

Freak-out No. 3. I can't do all this touchy-feely stuff, it feels like fluff to me.

Yes, it will feel like fluff to you because you are detail-driven and information-focused and this is big picture strategic planning. That's why this book is all about changing lives and revolutionising conversations in the accounting industry. Think of your own business as an example, or the business of a friend or family member. Is it non-emotional to them? Absolutely not. Think about how many times you've had clients upset in your office, and that was just when you were talking about compliance – although tax tends to make most people cry. You can do this. You already are doing it. You didn't just get up and walk away from your clients when they started to get emotional or talk about non-accounting or tax issues with their businesses, did you? It might have been uncomfortable but you did it because you care about your clients and their wellbeing in general. With this book you have an amazing system and a plethora of tools to help you engage in these conversations with your clients in a structured way. There's no looking back.

You'll be very happy to know that is the last of the three big implementation chapters. The reading gets much easier from here on in. In the next chapters, I elaborate on the next two levels of Leading Edge Business™: PROTECT and POSITION.

Actions to Take After Reading This Chapter

1. Download the PLAN Agendas.

2. Watch Our Plan for Today Video.

3. Download the PLAN Bonus Questions.

Additional Information/Resources

- PLAN Client Agenda

- PLAN Detailed Agenda

- PLAN Bonus Questions

- Our Plan for Today Video.

You will find the links to download all the documents listed under the above two headings here: https://lyndasteffens.com/bonuses

9

PROTECT and POSITION

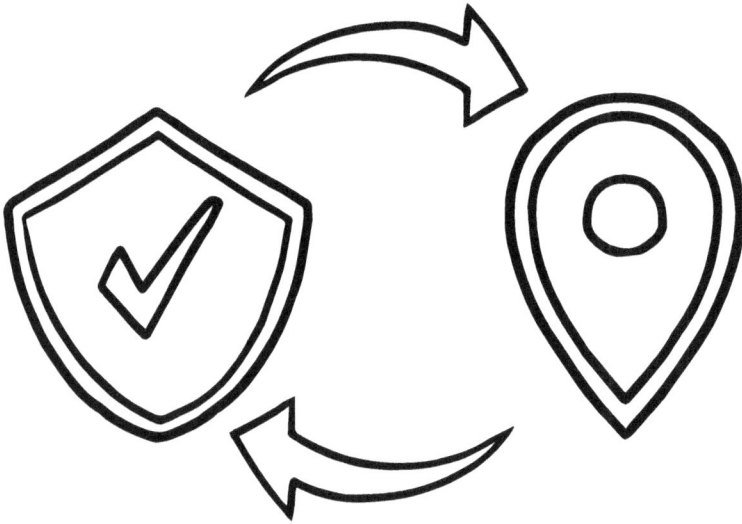

Be real and adjust your strategy against honest results
— Charles Caleb Colston[18]

---

18 Goodreads.com, 2019

Put simply, numbers don't lie and when used effectively they provide powerful insights into protecting a business and positioning it for growth. Your clients don't know this, you do, so you should do something about that, shouldn't you?

Show your clients the power of numbers and give them the best chance possible for succeeding in business. Using all the advisory services you already have in place, repurpose and repackage these advisory services into powerful business protection and positioning solutions. That's why you got into accounting in the first place, isn't it, to help people succeed in business? You have all the skills you need and a broad and extensive knowledge of how to use the power of numbers. Share it. Stop sitting back and waiting for clients to ask for advisory services. They don't know what they don't know. Take the initiative, get on the front foot, and make it happen.

Our clients are our why, the reason we do what we do, our number one motivation, so you should do everything in your power to bridge the gap from just playing a functional role in their businesses, providing tax returns and financials, to becoming a vital and ongoing part of their business journey. PROTECT and POSITION your clients as they tackle business growth. Be the supportive advisor and guiding light they have been looking for, providing them with regular guidance and support.

Share all your amazing superpowers and use them for good, not evil. Information, analysis, and your processing power are all things to be celebrated and exactly what your clients want in an advisor. Tackling the challenges of business ownership is scary and unrelenting. Educate and support your clients with the power of numbers and increase their business skills base.

Revel in your conservative and low-risk nature. Use it to its best advantage. This is how you roll. Don't let your clients get caught up in all the false promises and marketing about improving their businesses tenfold overnight. There are no overnight successes. Just check and you'll find most 'overnight' success stories were at least

10 years in the making. Set your clients on the right path, protecting and positioning their business ready for growth and success, and be there with the right advice when they need you.

Availability and approachability are the top two reasons people leave their accountants.

> *Talent is great but being in the right place at the right time is better*
> — *Endale Edith*[19]

If you continue to sit back and wait for your clients to ask for advisory services and opportunities for the work you love, you'll be waiting a long time to grow your business, if ever, forcing you to continue with the daily grind of compliance. Failing to help clients when they need advice will almost certainly ensure, as an industry, that we become dinosaurs, irrelevant and extinct because we did not move with the times, facing the real fear that comes with failing in our duty of care.

You've made it through all the hard stuff and are now on the home stretch. This chapter is a much shorter and lighter read. It's all about giving insight into which advisory services fit within the Leading Edge Business™ levels PROTECT and POSITION. In previous chapters, I've spoken at length about the flexibility of the Leading Edge Business™ model. You'll see all this flexibility and more come to the fore in this chapter. The best part is you can have all this flexibility without losing an inch of structure. I'll show you how. With the development of The Small Business Project, I never set out to tell accountants how to do their jobs, or what types of advisory services they should provide. Of course, I make recommendations but ultimately those decisions are up to you, you are in control. The objective of The Small Business Project and the Accounting Revolution program is to help you unleash your superpowers,

---

19 Goodreads.com, 2019

allowing you to instantly connect with your clients in a way that makes you money simply by changing your conversations. The Small Business Project is the engagement piece, the structure, the tools, the scripts, the knowledge, and the HOW to help you do all of that. So, let's get cracking and show you how to incorporate Leading Edge Business™ into your business.

P2: PROTECT

PROTECT is the second level of Leading Edge Business™. It's all about collaboratively working with your client to protect their business using the power of numbers.

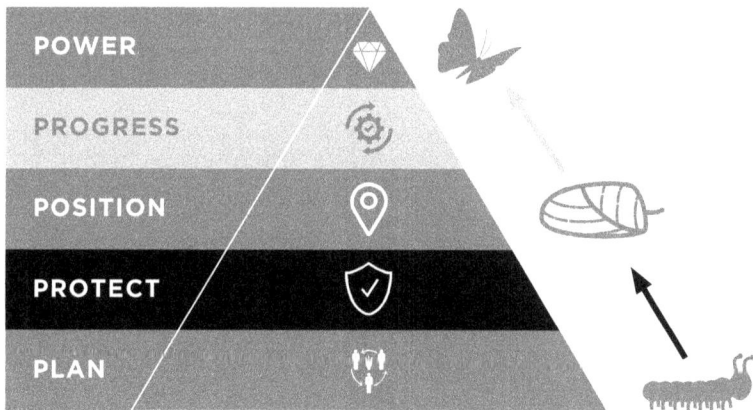

Figure 9.1 The 5Ps and PROTECT

I've always had a bent towards learning, and by extension teaching. It's been right from when I played schools as a child and wanted to be a teacher, through to my first accounting business where educating my clients about tax was forefront, evidenced by my tagline 'Teaching you the Truth about Tax'. It continues now on my speaking and coaching journey.

PROTECT is very much about learning and teaching, giving your client all the tools they need to PROTECT their business. Almost always when someone in the financial industry talks about protecting something, they mean some type of insurance. Not so in this case. PROTECT has two main objectives: (1) to ensure your client's data is clean, correct, timely, and reliable, and (2) to educate your client about the power of numbers, what to look at, when to look at them, and what they are telling you.

Objective One: Clean, Correct, Timely, Reliable Data

You and I both know that to harness the power of numbers and the power of advisory offerings, the story the numbers are telling needs to be correct and we require timely access to that story. Incorrect data means incorrect analysis, incorrect assumptions, and therefore incorrect decisions. No data at all means you're flying blind and going on gut feel. Neither of these situations bodes well for business success but get the numbers right, and you've got some formidable information to work with.

Advisory services that meet PROTECT's first objective would be things like:

- Bookkeeping audits

- Bookkeeping quarterly reviews

- Full-service bookkeeping

- Bookkeeping training and support.

As an aside, I'm seeing the term 'bookkeeping' increasingly being replaced by 'data management', and 'bookkeepers' referred to as 'data managers'. The argument is that no-one is keeping books anymore but rather managing data. Time will tell if this sticks.

You'll recall the simplest definition of advisory services is anything that's not compliance, so bookkeeping or data management as a service, training, and support fall well within your advisory capacity. In fact, it's integral. Get the numbers wrong, or get no numbers at all, and a business has nowhere to go. It's as simple as that. Educate your clients about investing time and resources in their numbers because if they are serious about growing their business, as boring as it might sound, this is the place they need to start. Who said owning a business was all fun and games? Work with them, teaching and showing them that numbers don't lie and when used effectively, they provide powerful insights into protecting and positioning a business for growth. It's the insurance that should be compulsory for every business.

My partner started a business for the first time a couple of years ago, having always been an employee. His family were not businesspeople and he had never been involved in business himself. One of the first things I taught him was how to do his own bookkeeping. It took a couple of years, a fair amount of cursing, and a lot of 'why can't a bookkeeper do this?' but he now understands and sees the importance of this step as part of his business journey. We've used the power of numbers to help him with decision-making over the years and he is now a true convert (regardless of the odd bout of swearing from time to time).

Objective Two: The Power of Numbers

This is purposefully centred around education. Numbers don't mean anything unless you have an appreciation of what you're looking at and more to the point, what they are telling you. Your No. 2 Superpower, Analysis, is what kicks into gear for this step. Assisting your clients to develop and monitor meaningful KPIs is a great place to start. This doesn't need to be anything fancy. Simply monitoring turnover levels and gross profit margins on an ongoing basis is a great way to get started. You'll recollect I've said you have all the tools you need. You might just be taking them for granted. Monitoring these two simple and readily available KPIs will give both you and your client insights into their business that could be vital to their success. We know that you can't operate a business that is costing more to run than what you make, but the first our clients often know about it is when they can't pay the BAS, then the wages, and so on, until in the worst-case scenarios, they end up in bankruptcy. We should help our clients with this stuff, use our superpowers for good not evil, shouldn't we?

Advisory services that meet PROTECT's second objective would be things like:

- Cashflow budgets

- KPI development

- Breakeven analysis

- Cashflow monitoring

- KPI monitoring and accountability

- Pricing and costing

- Chart of account reviews

- How to read financial reports.

Think about this list as being eight months' worth of topics for your Leading Edge Business™ program. Cover a topic a month in monthly meetings with your clients. Business owners and your clients are screaming out to be educated and trained in basic business management, so much so they are looking for others like business coaches and consultants to help them when the best person to help them is right under their noses. They suspect it, hope for it, and want you to do it. You just need to make it happen.

As an accountant, I love information and when I was developing PROTECT I was thinking about arming business owners with all the information they need for business success. Forewarned is forearmed, is it not? Therefore, in PROTECT, you could work with your clients on developing meaningful KPIs for their business, help them monitor those KPIs, help them analyse and interpret them, all the while educating them and improving their business skills and paving the road to business success. Easy and simple things you take for granted, like explaining the importance of the layout of your client's chart of accounts so they get the information they need at a glance, how to read the P&L and balance sheet, monitoring cashflow and being accountable for KPIs like turnover and profit margins.

We tend to want to get all fancy and make offering advisory services hard and complicated, thinking this is where our value lies. It doesn't. It's the simple stuff our clients want, simple for us but it's far from simple for them.

Once you have their bookkeeping or data management looked after, the first thing I would consider doing for your clients is developing a cashflow budget and monitoring major KPIs like turnover, gross profit, and net profit margins, even if the numbers might be a little off kilter initially. It will only take a brief 15 to 20-minute monthly conversation with your client to put this type of accountability and knowledge in place. You don't personally need to do it. This is a great way to get your team involved with The Small Business Project. They can be doing these accountability touch bases using internet meeting platforms like Zoom and Skype for business. Think about it. It only takes a few minutes to look at the client's management accounts for the month and plug the results into an Excel template. If you wanted to get all fancy (and there is certainly no need to so don't overcomplicate it), you could produce some basic graphs, presenting the information in a visual format to make it easier for your client to digest it, then simply sit down and have a phone or Zoom conversation with them.

 A coach is not an 'expert' but a facilitator of learning.

Remember: you are not an expert in everyone's business and neither should you be. You are, however, an expert in the mechanics of business and when it all boils down, the big picture dynamics of business and HOW to use the power of numbers to predict, analyse, and PROTECT are the same for all businesses. Teach your client to fish, don't just give them the fish. Encourage their resourcefulness by working with them on KPIs. The interpretation of KPIs and the monitoring of them is the power of PROTECT. Availability and approachability are the top two reasons people leave their accountants. With The Small Business Project, there will be no more lack of availability and approachability for you.

P3: POSITION

POSITION is the third level of Leading Edge Business™. It's all about getting your client's business in the right place ready to tackle growth initiatives.

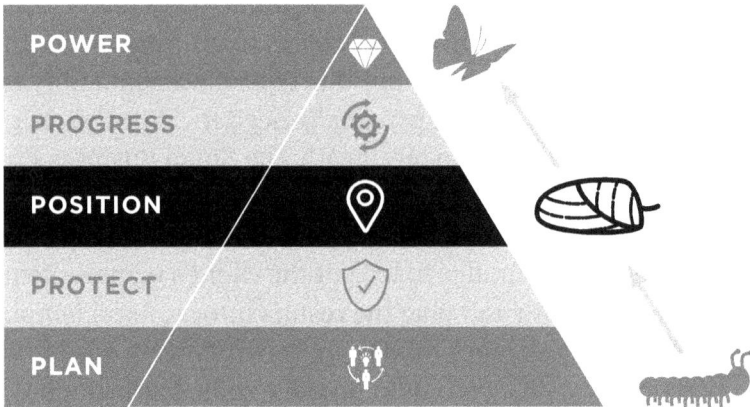

Figure 9.2 The 5Ps and POSITION

How many times have clients come to you desperately needing help because their business has had the most amazing growth spurt, which has ultimately resulted in absolute chaos both financially and emotionally? Knowing you cannot separate life and business, and therefore the emotion of business, is a great leveller, so get with the program. Leading Edge Business™ and POSITION allow you to get on the front foot and hopefully avoid these desperate grabs for help when often it's already too late. You don't need the stress, and neither do your clients, and they will happily pay you to avoid it.

If you haven't already worked it out, Leading Edge Business™ and the 5Ps allow you to communicate value to your clients in a structured way and on an ongoing basis. They give you the infrastructure to talk to clients directly about WHY they should invest in their business and partner with you to show them HOW.

PLAN, PROTECT, and POSITION are just the start of the journey.

The objective of POSITION is to ready your client's business for growth and even though some of the services will be the same as PROTECT, it has a different focus. POSITION's focus is on growth and the financial impact of growth on your client's business.

Advisory services that meet POSITION'S objective and growth focus would be things like:

- Cashflow forecasting
- Financial modelling
- Virtual CFO
- Pricing and costing
- What-if analysis
- Systems and procedures
- Tax structuring
- Tax planning
- HR compliance
- Finance applications
- Capital raising

Business owners need to understand the implications of growth and what that can mean for their businesses. I saw growth getting the better of a business time and time again when I was in practice.

It was often too late for me to help and I had nothing in my toolbox to even attempt to alert my clients and ward off the devastating circumstances. Leading Edge Business™ gives you the structure and the opportunity to get on the front foot. Preparing your clients financially for the burdens of growth using services like pricing, financial modelling, what-if analysis, and forward cashflow forecasting, all tools you already have in your toolbox, is one of the best things you can do.

So, what does positioning a business look like? When I'm working with accountants, I like to explain this by using a story about building a superhighway.

Think about a superhighway. Traffic generally flows smoothly on these roads if the volume of traffic matches the capacity of the road. To enable sustainable growth, your business needs a better road that can handle more traffic travelling at higher average speeds consistently: the superhighway. At the moment, you're bumping along a one-lane dirt road that has not been maintained very well and is not in top shape. What would happen if you forced more cars to travel along this road without making any changes or upgrading it? Traffic jams and traffic accidents would be commonplace, and eventually cars might stop using the road and find alternative routes. In order to grow, you need the superhighway and you need it in place and ready for cars. You start by upgrading the dirt road and making improvements, increasing your road infrastructure always a little in front of when you need it. The road and superhighway are your systems and procedures, and the financial and management capacity to grow. The cars are your clients and your team members. Using the power of numbers and your superpowers, you can quite accurately predict when and what upgrades you'll require.

Use this story with your clients. It's very powerful. As an accountant, you have the ability to change lives. Do not underestimate this. Helping businesses with the many challenges associated with business growth, cashflow, efficiency, quality, turnaround times, and output will avoid a huge amount of stress for your clients. Helping your clients to understand HOW to get their business ready for growth before they start growing is the smart thing to do. You know that growing pains, at their worst, can be fatal for businesses. You probably have a few horror stories to share with your clients to help them understand.

Use storytelling to help your clients understand and learn.

POSITION clearly sits within the chrysalis phase of the Business Metamorphosis® model. See how it ties in with the business owner's focus. They need to be onto quality and process (the road and infrastructure), because when they want to grow their business they soon realise they need to add more people, and adding more people (cars) needs upgrades and money (to fund the road upgrades). Additionally, when they add more people to their business, particularly if it happens to be the first time they're adding someone, there is a real risk that the quality of their product and/ or service will be affected. They can't control people but they can control process, the communication of their strategic goals, and the performance levels they want to uphold.

Your client will have all this information from undertaking PLAN, PROTECT, and POSITION and it will take them a long way to managing quality and efficiency as they grow. This may also be the first time your client steps into the manager role. They will need your ongoing support and guidance, which you can deliver through monthly touch base and accountability meetings.

A coach is not an 'expert' but a facilitator of learning.

You may find your client is on a similar growth journey to you. Don't be afraid to draw on your joint experiences to facilitate learning for you both. Allowing yourself to be vulnerable will enhance the learning experience for both you and your client. Don't take the arrogant road of the expert and act as if you know everything. I don't know about you, but when I got my first opportunity to do tax returns in front of clients, the advice that was driven home to me was that if I didn't know something I should say, let the client know that I would find out for them, reassuring them that I would get the right answer and the best result for them. Thanks to that advice very early in my career, I've always felt comfortable saying I don't know stuff. It's stood me in good stead as an advisor and now as a coach. Thank you, Mr T.

A reminder: there is no set timeframe for how long your clients spend at any one of the 5Ps. It will always depend on your client and their journey. One client may need a lot more help to get their data reliable in PROTECT before moving onto POSITION. Their cashflow may not allow it, or they may not yet be willing to move at a faster pace. There will be other clients who are.

Flexibility to Increase Services

If a client wants to move faster, don't be afraid to increase the level of the service and their financial commitment. They might want to meet with you fortnightly rather than monthly to get a new initiative cracking along. Coaches always ensure they have flexibility in their diaries to ensure a client can scale up or down their level of commitment.

That's a wrap on P2: PROTECT and P3: POSITION.

Leading Edge Business™ is not about telling you how to do accounting and tax. It's giving you the infrastructure to communicate value to your clients on an ongoing basis about your advisory services and tools, allowing you to put them together in a client journey that they will both want and value.

After reading this chapter, you might be thinking that you don't have all these advisory services in place and ready to go. Does that mean you can't do these levels with clients? Absolutely not. Leading Edge Business™ is flexible enough to allow you to interpret the levels in any way you wish and to suit whatever current advisory offerings you have on hand. The example services I've used in the chapter are not set in stone. Be smart about using strategic alliances to deliver services you don't currently offer or don't ever envisage offering. And remember, like attracts like, so your clients are likely to be at a similar or lesser stage of business than you. By the time they are ready for the services, you'll be ready to deliver them.

You might also be thinking that there doesn't seem to be a clear distinction between P2: PROTECT and P3: POSITION. Some of the services overlap and there is no clear way of defining when you move from one to another. You're right, there isn't. That's part of the flexibility of the model. It's designed to flow seamlessly between the levels. You can see that PROTECT and POSITION go hand in hand. The advisory services used in these levels may well be the same but they have a different focus: PROTECT the fundamentals of business management and POSITION preparing for business growth.

But you're not an expert in everyone's business. How will you know what your client needs to do to move from PROTECT and into POSITION? You're right again, you guys are so smart. You're not experts in everyone's business and it's not up to you to be an expert in every one of your client's businesses. What you are an expert in and where your superpowers lie is in business mechanics: the fundamentals and general underlying principles of what make businesses succeed. Using your superpowers for good and imparting this knowledge to your clients, delivering it using all the power of numbers, is life-changing.

Just had a last-minute thought. Think of the power of numbers like Thor's hammer. It's your connection to your superpowers. Use it and use it wisely, as Obi-Wan Kenobi would say.

Actions to Take After Reading This Chapter

1. Download the Leading Edge Business™ Services Template.

2. Add your services for P2: PROTECT to the Leading Edge Business™ Services Template.

3. Add your services for P3: POSITION to the Leading Edge Business™ Services Template.

Additional Information/Resources

- Leading Edge Business™ Services Template.

You will find the links to download all the documents listed under the above two headings here: https://lyndasteffens.com/bonuses

10

PROGRESS and POWER

All progress takes place outside the comfort zone

— Michael John Bobak[20]

P4: PROGRESS

PROGRESS is the fourth level of Leading Edge Business™. The objective of PROGRESS is to move your client forward and help them to stay on track with their plans and initiatives. PROGRESS has a strong accountability component.

Complete your transition from just being functional, delivering tax returns and financials to your clients, by evolving into a vital part of your clients' businesses, working collaboratively with your clients on profitable projects of high value where they want and value your input and accept your guidance. Help your clients to future-proof their businesses and take them to the next level. Realise your accounting potential by becoming an accountant of the now and of the future. This is truly the revolution.

Half of all professional services employees worry that technology will make their skills and knowledge less valuable.

> *The best time to plant a tree was 20 years ago. The second-best time is now* — *Chinese proverb*[21]

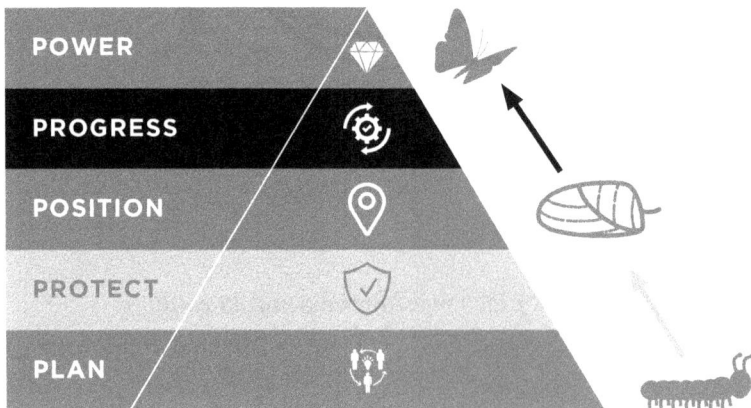

Figure 10.1 The 5Ps and PROGRESS

---

21 Psychology Today, 2019

Action and accountability are the key features of PROGRESS. We'll get to accountability a little later. PROGRESS relies on some of the same advisory services incorporated into P2 and P3. You couldn't have possibly missed me raving on and on about Leading Edge Business™ being super-flexible and designed to be adaptable to all accounting businesses and their advisory service offerings, including whether those advisory service offerings are extensive or not. Each P has its own distinctive objective or objectives. These objectives determine how you use your advisory service. For example, cashflow budgeting as an advisory service fits perfectly well within P2, P3, P4, and P5 for that matter. You can use cashflow budgeting to deliver the specific objective of the P level you are working in. Examples: In P4: PROGRESS you can use it to determine the financing requirements of a business as they PROGRESS with their growth initiatives. In P2: PROTECT you can use it to balance turnover, overheads, and cashflow requirements to PROTECT the business from assuming too much debt, which can ultimately lead to bankruptcy.

PROGRESS is centred on the action of moving your client forward with their plans and initiatives, and the accountability of doing that.

Advisory services that meet the objective and focus of PROGRESS are things like:

- Virtual CFO

- Board of advice

- Monthly accountability meetings

- Cashflow monitoring & budgeting

- KPI development

- KPI monitoring

- HR management

- Leadership training

- Marketing.

How to Get Started with PROGRESS

The first thing is to create a list of agreed initiatives you and your client decide to work collaboratively on. Monitor expected timelines for those initiatives and how you will measure the success of each so you know when your client has achieved their goals. You can see how important developing and putting into place KPIs are for this phase.

A quick word about setting PROGRESS goals. You want your client to be able to achieve their goals within six to nine months (perhaps 12 months at a stretch). Any timeframe beyond that and it's difficult to maintain traction. For example, your client's 10 out of 10 business might have a $10 million turnover. If they're currently turning over $2 million, you wouldn't want to make the next step $10 million. Perhaps $2.5 million or $3 million, depending on the industry, would be much more appropriate. In any case, the initiatives you'd be running to take a business from $2 million to $3 million, versus taking a $7 million business to a $10 million business, would be vastly different. Remember: there are no set timeframes for how long you stay within a phase, but clear advancement and achievement of goals is necessary. Set PROGRESS goals that are manageable within a six to 12-month timeframe. When you achieve them, refocus, realign, and set new PROGRESS goals, or move to P5.

You want to align the initiatives with the overall strategic focus and your client's 10 out of 10 business, always moving them closer to that outcome. The PROGRESS plan and initiatives are never written in stone so don't think you need to have them perfect before you start. From time to time, you may find you have to change tack.

P4: PROGRESS and its initiatives are as flexible as they need to be. Then it's all down to accountability. Accountability! Phooey, you say, what's so great about that? Well, it has 'account' in it and you're an accountant. Coincidence? I think not, but perhaps the most important result of accountability is trust. Being accountable to something or someone means that you're willing to make commitments and be responsible for your own actions. You know that trying to deliver services to clients who do not wish to be accountable is like pushing the proverbial uphill.

Accountability is the most powerful of coaching methodologies.

The easiest and most effective way to run accountability is the use of action plans.

Meetings Need Action Plans

In any meeting you're keeping an Action Plan. Action plans need detail:

a. What the action is – be clear and concise

b. When the action is to be completed by

c. Who is responsible for completing the action.

And remember the way you start any meeting? With The Coach Approach, focusing on the why.

Focus on the Why

Every meeting starts by revisiting:

1. Your client's Business Metamorphosis® gap, from caterpillar to butterfly

2. Your client's DISCOVER gap. 'You were a five. We're working towards a 10'

3. Your client's PLAN strategic foundation. Their vision, mission, values, and target market.

This structure and focus on the why reinforces the value of the Leading Edge Business™ process for your client at each and every meeting. It also keeps you focused on the overall outcomes, making it easy for you to align and plan initiatives in the PROGRESS phase.

PROGRESS is also the level where movement between Business Metamorphosis® phases can become very apparent. You should always capitalise on this fact when you meet with your client.

Continue to use Business Metamorphosis® as your guiding force. This is yet another important reason for incorporating this model every time you meet with your client.

When a client moves between Business Metamorphosis® stages, particularly the caterpillar to chrysalis phase where their job goes from that of a doer to a manager, they may start to question their value to the business. If you think about it for a second, they were used to doing everything their business needed done and were 100% active in generating their cashflow, so they saw their value directly correlated with cashflow. As their role changes to manager, that correlation weakens and they may question the process. It's easy enough to guide your client through this transition, so let me tell you Nik's story.

At the time we were working on growing his business, Nik was a website builder. He wanted to move into a business development and leadership role rather than being the doer and building websites. He used to joke and refer to himself as a grub rather than a caterpillar. Caterpillars rule. Nik had expanded his team from just himself and one other to include a manager, several technicians, and marketing and administration virtual assistants. The next step was client relationship and operations managers. He was struggling with what value he was delivering to the business. He didn't feel important anymore because he hadn't built a website in months. I whipped out the Business Metamorphosis® model and reiterated to him where he had been when we first started working together and how he had come such a long way in such a short time. Showing him that his role and therefore what value he brought to the business had changed and must continue to change in order for us to deliver the future he wanted worked a treat and we got Nik back on track.

Empower and motivate clients by showing them how far they have come, using the Business Metamorphosis® and Leading Edge Business™ models to illustrate their journey and tell their story.

P5: POWER

POWER is the fifth and final level of Leading Edge Business™. The objective of this level is for your clients to feel they have taken back POWER over their business. Many small business owners feel their businesses control them rather than the other way around. POWER holds great value for them, allowing them to stay in charge. The focus of POWER is to future-proof your client's business and take it to the next level, whatever that may be for them.

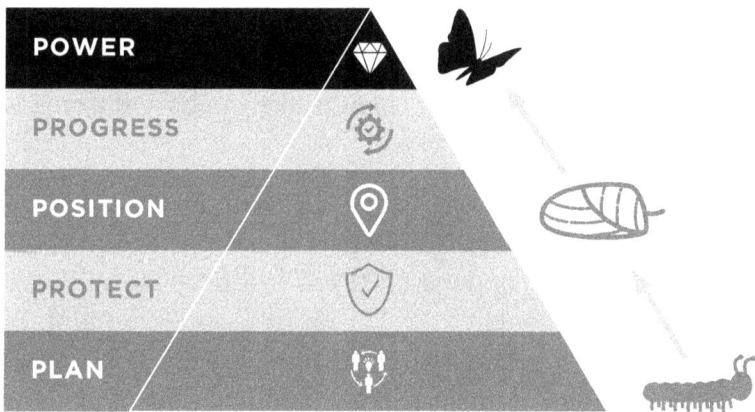

Figure 10.2 The 5Ps and POWER

Advisory services that meet the objective and focus of POWER are things like:

- Wealth creation
- Financial planning
- SMSF advisory
- Succession planning
- Estate planning
- Board of advice.

POWER is the level where you can get creative, helping your client realise goals and ambitions they never thought possible.

Hang on, hang on! You're an accountant. You don't have a creative bone or molecule in your body, do you? Maybe, maybe not, but you have superpowers and your hammer, and the power of numbers to help with future-proofing. Your client is likely to have the creative stuff already planned out for you.

An accounting client recently told me she wanted to do a TED talk (these are influential videos from expert speakers on education, business, science, tech, and creativity). It surprised me a little, as it wasn't something I thought I would hear from an accountant. But then, getting over myself and thinking about my client, I realised it suited her perfectly. Next level will be different for everyone. One client's next level might be to work back through Leading Edge Business™ with bigger and better turnover and profitability goals in place. Another's might be building a rocket and taking passengers into space, like Richard Branson. Who knows? Your job is just to ask and find out what it is.

Facilitating not Participating

You're asking questions, not providing answers.

You don't and won't know the answers.

Information is power and using it to work with your clients to understand their future and help them protect it is just about as influential and powerful as it comes. POWER is the final level of Leading Edge Business™ but it is not the end. With every new growth initiative your client would like to tackle, it's just the leverage to loop right back around and work through the 5Ps and all levels again. Using the Business Metamorphosis® journey from caterpillar to butterfly to anchor your client's journey, and then adding in Leading Edge Business™ to deliver your advisory services and work with your clients on an ongoing basis to deliver their 10 out of 10 is highly rewarding and satisfying, wouldn't you say?

Wowee. How are you travelling? Can you see the light at the end of the tunnel? You might be able to see that light, but you're probably still a bit freaked out thinking you've never done accountability meetings before and you can't do them. Yes, you can, and all you need to do is use your positive mindset to overcome thinking like that. I bet you skim-read Chapter 6 Find Your Superpowers, didn't you? You'd better go back and read it more thoroughly. It has all the answers.

Your value to all those around you is not in answers. It is clearly and undeniably in questions.

But wait, you're already taking clients on this journey. If you think about it, you've already worked with your client on advisory services that PROTECT, POSITION, PROGRESS, and give POWER. You might even do some of the PLAN elements.

But just take an objective look at the clients that you have undertaken the advisory journey with. I'd say there is a very good chance that your clients only engaged with your advisory services on an ad hoc basis, jumping from service to service as they thought they needed them. These were more than likely your A-class clients where cashflow and money were not a concern. There was no structure or model to the journey, in fact it wasn't really a journey, just a hop-on hop-off bus scenario where you were reactive to your client's needs.

The main goal of Leading Edge Business™ is the expression of value to show your client their business journey and what working together looks like. It's a client engagement model showing your client what's next in the journey, keeping them focused on the ultimate goal, their 10 out of 10. It aims to truly engage your clients in the process of delivering advisory services and helps you keep them engaged on an ongoing basis.

You might also be thinking, hold your horses Lynda, clients won't pay for accountability meetings. You've tried the service before and it never got off the ground. When you previously tried to introduce accountability meetings, you most likely failed to engage the client in any type of process so they understood:

- what they were being accountable for

- why it was so important

- most importantly, what the overall goal was.

Use Business Metamorphosis® and the 3Ds and your client will be sufficiently engaged to take up accountability meetings as a service.

Clients will pay for accountability meetings. Why do you think the business coaching industry is so successful? Accountability is why. It's very difficult to continually motivate yourself and keep driving forward to deliver great results. Everyone needs help to do this and clearly, business owners are happy to pay for it. They just need to see the value and the journey. Don't worry. With The Small Business Project, you'll always deliver more than just accountability because with your collective knowledge and expertise, the value that you deliver to your clients by increasing their business skills and knowledge is simply invaluable.

So that's Leading Edge Business™ and the 5Ps, the second phase of The Small Business Project. I hope you have a very good understanding of the objectives and focus of each of the 5Ps by now. Be sure to leverage this information and take some time straightaway to apply Leading Edge Business™ to your practice. Prepare a suite of advisory services while it's all fresh in your mind.

If you feel you would like some more help, I hold regular Leading Edge Business™ workshops. Just go to my website https://lyndasteffens.com to check out when the next one is scheduled and book in.

The Small Business Project is a three-phase program designed to revolutionise the accounting industry and how you, as an accountant, engage with your clients.

Phase 1   Business Metamorphosis®

Phase 2   Leading Edge Business™

Phase 3   Ready Set Coach™

I've covered Phase 1 and Phase 2. Now let's get moving on Phase 3, Ready Set Coach™, and get your practice and team coaching ready.

Actions to Take After Reading This Chapter

1. Add your services for P4: PROGRESS to the Leading Edge Business™ Services Template.

2. Add your services for P5: POWER to the Leading Edge Business™ Services Template.

11

Ready Set Coach™

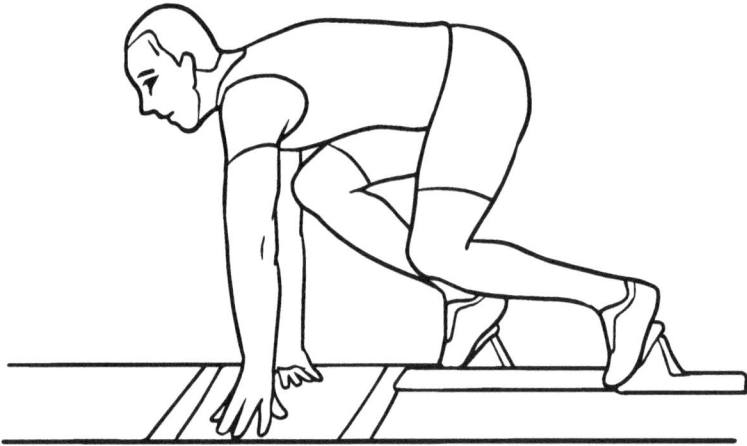

Make it your business to draw out the best in others by being an exemplar yourself

— *Epictetus*[22]

---

22 https://quotefancy.com/quote/802205/Epictetus-Make-it-your-business-to-draw-out-the-best-in-others-by-being-an-exemplar

WANTED: Motivated accountants who are keen to learn and want to do better for their clients. Get practice-ready with Ready Set Coach™.

Ready Set Coach™ is Phase 3 of The Small Business Project. It is specifically designed with accountants in mind. It is a four to six-month one-on-one coaching program designed to get you, your practice, and your team ready to deliver Business Metamorphosis® and Leading Edge Business™ to your clients.

It comprises four primary modules and a growing number of secondary optional modules. I will cover the four primary modules in this chapter.

Ready Set Coach™ is designed to be completed with a master facilitator and coach, like myself. It would not be easy to complete on your own as it would test all your leadership capabilities, but it is achievable. I promised I would hold nothing back. This wouldn't be a how-to book unless I shared Ready Set Coach™ with you.

Here's how you do it.

Before Starting Ready Set Coach™

Before you undertake Ready Set Coach™ I recommend you complete Business Metamorphosis® and the 3Ds. Embarking on The Small Business Project with my master coaches always starts with Business Metamorphosis®. We practise what we preach and it's important that do you as well.

Working through Ready Set Coach™ either by yourself or with one of my coaches gives you great storytelling content to use with your clients. Sharing your own story and journey will allow your clients to know, like, and trust you at supersonic speed. Think of it as a superpower upgrade.

Business Metamorphosis®

Chart yourself and your business on the Business Metamorphosis® interactive model. Print it out and do that now. Here's where you'll find it: https://lyndasteffens.com/bonuses

The 3Ds

1 DISCOVER

Understand your own gaps by sitting down with the DISCOVER script and openly and honestly answering the questions about your business. Note down particularly how it makes you feel to be where you are, and how it would make you feel if you stayed there and didn't improve. Remember: you must play full out for this exercise to work. Be 100% open and honest with yourself, otherwise you're wasting your time and you could be doing tax returns.

2 DIG

Perform your own DIG. Set goals and work towards realising those goals. Set some time aside to work through the agenda for your own business. This works best if you take time out of the office to do this, so that you are not tempted by your workload or get dragged back into the regular office goings-on.

3 DELIVER

Take your DIG Action Plan and schedule time over the next 90 days to complete the actions. Hold yourself accountable to the due dates. I find this works best if you start by setting aside one afternoon a week to work **on** your business rather than working **in** your business. Schedule this time in your calendar and ask your team to help you remain accountable to working on the business by asking them not to book any client appointments at that time. It's important you give them permission to do this. If they need to ask you every time a client requests an appointment during your 'working on' your business time, you know you'll cave to the client's request. I know you will and you know you will too. We're service people and we can't help it.

Don't Set Yourself up to Fail

Give yourself plenty of time, be prepared, gather information, follow the system, practise, and pick an easy target. By that I mean don't try to block out time for working **on** your business when you know it will be busy. For instance, Thursday afternoons might be your usual client appointment day, your appointments usually run over, and you need to leave early to take your children to sport. Clearly, you need to pick a different day.

Once you've nailed sticking to one afternoon, then try for two afternoons a week, maybe even more, depending on the size of your business and what role you want to undertake.

During Ready Set Coach™

Module 1 – Strategic Foundation (PLAN)

Create your own strategic foundation. Go back to Chapter 8 The Master Plan and implement everything in the chapter for your own business. Did you skim-read it? If you did here's your chance to rectify that. There is no way it will work if you try to do your own PLAN session in bits and pieces, squeezing in a little bit here, a little bit there. You need to immerse yourself in the process, just like you do when you undertake it with a client. Schedule time in your diary to conduct your own PLAN session AWAY from the office with plenty of time to think. I recommend a full day.

Don't be fooled. Doing this for yourself will be tricky. This PLAN session will be one of the hardest you'll ever do. Be diligent in following the process. Use the scripts, Bonus Questions, and all the 'Tricks of the Trade'. If you're successful in doing your own, there is no client who will ever thwart you.

Just Start

As accountants, we naturally analyse everything and then analyse it again to be sure. There's no 80/20 for us, it's 100% or nothing.

Challenge yourself and just start. It won't be perfect but you'll have started.

Module 2 – Operational Excellence (PROTECT)

Here's where you start to involve your team. Download the agenda so you know what's involved. You start by discussing business, the business of accounting, and the future of the accounting industry. The purpose of this is to have your team focusing on you as a business, just like for any of your business clients. Discuss the big picture, namely, what's up and coming for the accounting industry and the challenges the future may present. Use the chapters in this book to help you out.

You then move onto explaining the Ready Set Coach™ Workflow. This is a best practice workflow for the core operations of an accounting practice.

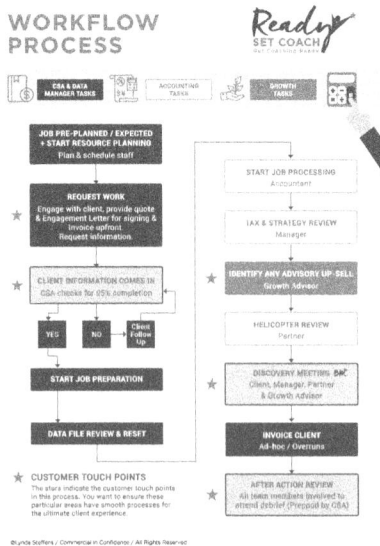

Figure 11.1 RSC Workflow Process

Next is the SWOT analysis where you brainstorm your strengths, weaknesses, opportunities, and threats around the key operational areas of your accounting business:

- Client Service

- Client Administration

- Software and Hardware

- Business Administration

- Workflow and Job Management

- Timesheets and Billing.

The objective of Module 2 is the creation of an Action Plan and the focus is improvement. This is an Action Plan of issues, pain points, and improvements that need to be worked on at a later date. You will not be spending time solving problems or making improvements on the spot. The mood is positive not negative.

Meetings Need Action Plans

In any meeting you're keeping an Action Plan. Action plans need detail.

a. What the action is – be clear and concise.

b. When the action is to be completed by.

c. Who is responsible for completing the action.

There can be a lot of fear around taking a good hard look at your business and opening yourself up to feedback from your team. It's normal and natural. Most of us don't do it simply because we're afraid of what we'll find out, and we think we'll just create a bigger mess.

It's okay, you've got this. Think of it like cleaning out a messy drawer. You start by pulling everything out of the drawer, then you work through each item, throwing things out that you don't need anymore, putting aside things that belong in other drawers, adding things that make sense to this drawer, and finally putting everything back in neatly and tidily. And guess what? Your tidy drawer has more space, more capacity for more things. You will always make a bigger mess before you get a clean and tidy result. Just like cleaning out drawers, it's an ongoing process. Things will get messy again and you will need to clean again.

Doing this stuff for yourself will be tricky, so a word of caution. Watch out the session does not turn into a 'let's solve the problems now' session, trying to solve issues, pain points, and make improvements. You're a solution-focused technician and so is your team, so it's natural they will try to do this, but you'll be there for a week if you allow this to happen. The SWOT analysis is not the time or place to be solving problems. You will need to set aside additional time to do that. Perhaps you only need a couple of team members involved in the initial stages. This is when you need to put your facilitator hat on and keep the session on track. Use the Action Plan to help you do this.

Set and communicate the meeting expectations right from the beginning. You can do this by including the objectives in the initial invitation to the team, and again when opening the meeting.

Schedule time in the calendar to review the operations with your team and let everyone have a chance to tell you what's happening and to express their thoughts and ideas. Remember: the focus of the meeting is improvement and the mood is positive. Keep a keen eye on the mood of the session. This session in particular can quickly spiral down into a blame game and 'everything is wrong'. This happens because it may be the first time the team have been given a chance to speak up. They will vent, and there are always those with a negative viewpoint. In fact, expect it and you'll spot it and pull it up quickly. Use the Pineapple Effect to help you out – see below.

The Pineapple Effect

Someone in the team needs to play devil's advocate for the SWOT to be effective. That may be you or a team member, but someone needs to challenge the status quo. Not in a mean-spirited way but in a 'how can we improve' way. I call feedback given in a positive light, and 100% focused on improvement, 'pineappling' or the 'Pineapple Effect'. I use the analogy of a pineapple because for most of us, giving feedback and constructive criticism is difficult to do. It doesn't feel nice. However, if the feedback comes from a positive place, a 'how can we improve' place, then it's a very necessary thing.

Think of it like a pineapple. It's hard, prickly, pokey, and rough on the outside. It doesn't look or feel nice but inside is a beautiful, juicy, sweet, bright yellow centre that you enjoy. Positive feedback delivered with the objective of making things better is like a pineapple: get past the prickly bit and it's very worthwhile.

What will be most difficult for you undertaking Module 2 – PROTECT on your own will be avoiding becoming defensive. You may have set up most of the systems yourself and feel as if you're being attacked when your team criticise them. Stay calm, don't go on the defensive, and ask some great questions.

Facilitating not Participating

You're asking questions, not providing answers.

You don't and won't know the answers.

Module 3 – Team Surveys (POSITION)

This module focuses on getting the team on board, engaging them in your journey, and positioning your accounting practice ready for growth. You do this by asking your team for their feedback using a questionnaire or survey, and then discussing the answers in a one-to-one meeting. The objective is to give your team the opportunity to give you feedback openly and honestly one to one.

Again, receiving this information can be quite confronting so use the Tricks of the Trade from Module 2 to help you stay positive throughout the meetings. Don't get defensive and stay on track without trying to solve problems and issues on the spot. You can use my survey questions, add to them, or come up with your own.

These meetings are very different from the salary review or performance review meetings you may already conduct with your team annually. In those meetings the direction of feedback is generally from employer to employee. With these meetings, the direction of feedback is clearly employee to employer.

For the team survey process to be effective, you need the team to be 100% open and honest with you. They may harbour fears about their job security, upsetting you, speaking out, being labelled a troublemaker, etc. Addressing these concerns at the start of each one-to-one meeting will reassure your team and go a long way to getting the most out of this exercise.

Module 4 – Team Retreat (POSITION)

Module 4 works further on positioning your accounting practice for growth. You do this by holding a team retreat. What a magic word! It conjures up yoga and meditation by a resort pool, palm trees, sunshine, and relaxation. Hmmm, wouldn't that be lovely. Sorry to let you down but this staff retreat is not about that at all, although if you have the budget you can hold it wherever you want. Please just invite me.

The objective of the staff retreat and of Module 4 is to engage your team at a strategic level. Bring them on the journey and have them create their own strategic foundation for the practice, one they engage with. Use the PLAN Detailed Agenda from Chapter 8 The Master Plan to guide you. Ah, see? Another chance to rectify your skim-reading habits. Don't say I didn't warn you.

When you're facilitating your staff retreat, you'll find you will need to swap hats back and forth throughout the session from coach to business owner and back again.

Wearing Two Hats

To help you visualise the difference between accountant and coach when talking with your clients, say, 'I'm going to take off my accountant hat and put on my advisor/coach hat. Is that okay?' This will help you switch into The Coach Approach.

All the Tricks of the Trade in this chapter and Chapter 8 The Master Plan similarly apply to Module 4 so keep them handy and use them as you need them, especially:

A coach stimulates clients' self-discovery by asking powerful questions.

After Ready Set Coach™

Taking Action and Being Accountable

There is absolutely no point in rolling out Ready Set Coach™ with your team unless you have every intention of continuing to take action, being accountable, and setting time and resources aside to accomplish this.

Here are some suggestions that might help you out:

- Hold regular team meetings
- Ask everyone to help you be accountable
- Schedule time in your calendar
- Incorporate celebrations
- Make action plans visible

- Make strategic foundations visible

- Set realistic timeframes

- Work on the business.

Optional Modules

For an up-to-date list of my Ready Set Coach™ optional modules, head to my website: https://lyndasteffens.com

Tackling Ready Set Coach™ on your own will be challenging and I'm sure you'll have some concerns like 'this sounds too big and confronting to do on my own', 'I don't have time to do all of this'.

Yes, I agree, and there is always more help at hand so you can contact me at any time. The best way to do so is to complete the contact form on my website: https://lyndasteffens.com/contact-me/ One of my team will soon be in touch with you.

As a coach, I know that time and money are for the most part just excuses. If you truly want to transition your business and undertake The Small Business Project to learn how to instantly connect with clients in a way that makes you money, offering advisory services to all clients on a regular and ongoing basis and avoiding the reliance on compliance trap, then you will find time to incorporate all you have learned from my book into your business.

Remember to give yourself permission to start working **on** your business and not always **in** it. Always working **in** your business is unlikely to deliver the future you have in mind for yourself. Stop letting yourself, your team, your family, and your clients down. Take action and do something about it.

'The team is already apathetic about change. We've tried things before and failed to implement. This is just another thing that will end up on the shelf and make no difference whatsoever.'

Perhaps it's true that you have tried to implement other strategies and systems before and failed dismally. So get back on the horse and try again. This is your business and your future. I know my program works. Accountants thank me for saving their businesses. It's why I do what I do and why I developed The Small Business Project. I have 100% faith in it, 100% faith in my industry, the accounting industry, and 100% faith in you.

Okay, so now you know all about The Small Business Program and its three phases:

1. Business Metamorphosis®

2. Leading Edge Business™

3. Ready Set Coach™.

You've got your team on board, and the necessary information. You have the structure and knowledge you need ... How do you start telling clients about it? Great question. Let's get right onto that, shall we?

Actions to Take After Reading This Chapter

1. Set aside one afternoon per week and be accountable for working on your business.

2. Schedule time in your diary away from the office to complete your Business Metamorphosis®:

   DISCOVER – we recommend half a day

   DIG – we recommend a full day

   DELIVER – be guided by your Action Plan.

3. Schedule time in your diary away from the office to complete Ready Set Coach™ Module 1: Strategic Foundation – we recommend a full day.

4. Propose times with your team to complete Ready Set Coach™:

   Module 2: Operational Excellence – we recommend a full day

   Module 3: Team Surveys – you'll need 45 minutes to 1 hour per team member

   Module 4: Team Retreat – we recommend a full day.

Additional Information/Resources

- RSC Operational Excellence Agenda

- RSC Team Survey Questions

You will find the links to download all the documents listed under the above two headings here: https://lyndasteffens.com/bonuses

12

Step Up to Stand Out

People don't buy what you do, they buy why you do it

— Simon Sinek[23]

Marketing and sales can strike paralysing fear into the heart of an accountant. Let me show you why you need not be concerned.

In 2018, it was reported that the accounting industry grew more slowly than all other professional service categories, lagging behind by more than two percentage points (Hinge Research Institute, 2018).

It's pretty simple: without sales, business fails. Don't fail to educate your clients about your new initiative and the value you can now deliver.

So you think you can't sell? I didn't think I could write a book either. Just goes to show, you can do anything you set your mind to. The trick is finding your way, the way that works for you, and obstinately embracing that regardless of what others, including so-called industry experts, tell you. I am no sales or marketing expert, far from it. This chapter is not about either of those two things. It's about how to take all your superpowers along with the newly learned information and knowledge from my book and channelling it into delivering value to your clients and sharing with them this exciting development.

> I've learned that people will forget what you said, people will forget what you did, but people will never forget how you made them feel — *Maya Angelou*[24]

My opinion of sales is that it is really just being passionate about what you do, being clear about why you do what you do, doing it well, and being prepared to talk openly, honestly, and clearly about your services. We've long held misconceptions about sales. We haven't bothered to educate ourselves on the subject because it wasn't our thing. Sales is for extroverts. Wrong again. Read Matthew Pollard's book *The Introvert's Edge: How the Quiet and Shy can*

---

24 BrainyQuote, 2019

Outsell Anyone. It's a quick and easy read and well worth the time, even if all you do is skim-read it.

One of the misconceptions is that if we don't win every sale, then we suck at it. Let's investigate that a little further. You have been in an industry that for a very long time has had a captive market of clients purchasing services because they have to, services they don't understand and that require an expert to deliver. No-one including your clients will question this. When someone enquires about your services, they've often found you through a referral from someone else. So they were a hot lead. You pretty much just had to be nice to them and you would win them as a client. A little harsh do you think, or close to the truth? Somewhere along the line, the business landscape and the rules of the game have changed. Welcome to the era of choice, the digital and information age. In my experience, because of our captive markets, our conversion rates have typically been high. I remember telling someone years ago that if I could get a prospective client into the boardroom, I estimated I had a 95% chance of picking them up as a client. The point I'm trying to make and taking a long time coming to is we think high sales conversion rates are the norm and if we don't make almost every sale then we suck at sales. By educating ourselves about the sales process we'll find that it's simply a numbers game. We're numbers people so that suits us perfectly, right? Our focus has just been a little skewed. We'll come to this later when we set some goals.

Another misconception we have is that we can say something once and that's enough. We're highly detailed information people and we pay attention when people say things. Our clients or our teams for that matter aren't necessarily engaged when we're talking with them so our message can fall on deaf ears. Marketing 101: regular and consistent messaging is the key.

Right, so let's break this down. Sales is:

1. Being passionate about what you do

2. Being clear about your why

3. Doing what you do well

4. Being prepared

5. Being open, honest, and clear with messaging.

Guess what? You've got all of this in the bag.

I've just educated you on how to put together your strategic foundation. The process of producing you own master PLAN will without doubt ignite your passion and motivation for what you do if it's lagged a little. No. 1 Being passionate about what you do, complete. In PLAN, you develop your WHY, so that's No. 2. Being clear about your why, also done and dusted. I assume you are good at what you do, as you wouldn't last long in the accounting industry if you weren't. No. 3 Doing what you do well, check. No. 4 Being prepared. Your number one superpower is information. You were born prepared, but you need to be willing to be prepared for sales conversations. This links directly to No. 5 Being open, honest, and clear with messaging. I'm sure you are, but due to our quiet natures and our detailed focus we may be challenged a little by this one. My advice would be to spend some time preparing your sales messages. Be willing to work on these so they are clear and concise. It will give you the confidence to be open and willing to share them. Give yourself permission to spend time working on your business and not just in it.

I am a member of a local Business Networking International (BNI) chapter on the Gold Coast where I live and at every weekly meeting, every member stands and gives a 30-second sales presentation about their business. With only 30 seconds (smaller chapters have up to 60 secs but never more than that), my message must be clear, concise, and to the point to be effective. Being a part of this amazing networking organisation has forced me to focus on my sales messages, refining and honing them every single week. At the time of writing this book, I'd just clocked up three years of membership, about 150 weekly presentations. I still prepare my weekly presentation the night before. I write it down and practise it by timing myself and speaking aloud at least four or five times. I have no doubt my neighbours know that I'm revolutionising the accounting industry.

Speaking Aloud

Make sure you speak aloud when you practise. Don't just think about what you would say by running through it in your mind. While internal monologue is the accountant's go-to technique (we love to do things in our heads), it won't work for practising what to say. As an introvert, you'll struggle to produce the words when you need them if all you've done is think them through. The cat, the dog, or even the chair works well to practise on.

Okay, that's all well and good but what about some actionable items that we can get cracking on straightaway! You can get cracking on sales message preparation stuff straightaway, you know. Don't avoid it!

Don't Set Yourself up to Fail

Give yourself plenty of time, be prepared, gather information, follow the system, practise, and pick an easy target.

And the easy target is ... internal marketing. Educate and engage your team with your sales messages and marketing activities. They are an integral part of this journey and need to be involved.

A number of years ago I was a practice manager of an accounting firm that had almost 40 team members. I held a monthly team meeting where my number one goal was to educate and engage the team with the firm's initiatives, systems, and procedures. It didn't matter if they were operational, strategic, social, work, sales, or marketing related, they all counted and it was all internal marketing and team engagement.

If you do not already have a regular monthly team meeting in place, then I would highly recommend rectifying that. It's best if you can have an administration person facilitate and organise the meeting. You might need to get the process started but then you can hand it over.

You need an internal vehicle to keep up steady and consistent messaging. Just like external marketing, saying it once won't cut it. Use all the available opportunities you have at your disposal: morning teas, team meetings, workflow meetings, huddles, anytime you're getting together.

Talk about this great book you're reading, *Accounting Revolution*, and The Small Business Project, and WHY you think it's so important for everyone in the room. Just doing this is like my BNI weekly presentation. It will help you hone your messaging and perfect the art of delivery. Don't underestimate the value of a captive audience. Use it to practise your storytelling. Talk to your team about client and business wins and losses and what you have learned from them. They will love it.

Out of your Comfort Zone

Yes, this is new, yes, this is different, yes, it is foreign to you, and yes, it will take practice and effort.

Righto, let's tackle clients, both new and existing, by keeping it simple. There is no need to overwhelm yourself with sales and marketing initiatives when they are already built into the system itself. You have all the structure and scripts you need in this book to communicate your sales message. The products will sell themselves. Two very simple initiatives is all that you need:

Initiative No. 1: Introduce your clients to Business Metamorphosis® at every opportunity.

Wrap up all your meetings with Business Metamorphosis®. If clients are in the office dropping off work or signing their tax returns and other compliance forms, or have come in to seek your advice about something, introduce them to Business Metamorphosis®. Go back to Chapter 2 Business Metamorphosis® and revisit how you go about the introduction.

When you're introducing clients to Business Metamorphosis®, remember to switch hats.

Wearing Two Hats

To help you visualise the difference between accountant and coach when talking to clients, say, 'I'm going to take off my accountant hat and put on my advisor/coach hat. Is that okay?' This will help you switch into The Coach Approach.

Accountability is super-important, so set some goals to monitor your performance.

Don't Set Yourself up to Fail

Give yourself plenty of time, be prepared, gather information, follow the system, practise, and pick an easy target.

Start out nice and easy and concentrate only on introducing clients to Business Metamorphosis® and booking DISCOVER meetings/calls. There is no need to tackle anything further. That's the beauty of The Small Business Project. The system will take over from there.

Your accountability goals might look something like this:

- Introduce Business Metamorphosis® to three clients a week

- Book one DISCOVER meeting/call per month.

When you introduce your client to Business Metamorphosis® and they're really keen, don't be afraid to do a DISCOVER meeting right then and there if you both have the time. There is no need to book a second meeting but given your nature, I understand booking a second meeting/call time gives you time to prepare and you will naturally feel more comfortable doing it this way. In time, you'll have no trouble doing them on the spot.

Initiative No. 2: Hold a Client Information Night (or a series of them).

All you're doing here is introducing clients to Business Metamorphosis® on a group basis instead of one on one. Take the opportunity to invite select clients along and thank them for their custom. Keep it simple and small: 10 to 15 people in the room is plenty. In your presentation, talk about WHY you do what you do. Use your strategic foundation to stay consistent and tell them the story of what led you to introduce Business Metamorphosis® to them. Then introduce Business Metamorphosis®, get them involved, and have them complete the interactive BM model during the presentation. Make sure you have a call to action at the end, similar to if they would like to find out more they can book a DISCOVER call with you. Set aside a number of spots in your diary for DISCOVER calls in the coming week and have your admin team set them up on the spot with clients who are interested. Don't worry if no-one books a DISCOVER call. They will all go home and think about what you said and will more than likely speak to you at the next available opportunity.

The Client Information Night should take no longer than one to one-and-a-half hours at most. It will be easy to set up, low cost, and it will really punch above its marketing and sales weight. To help you further we've included a Client Information Night Checklist that we use.

Just Start

As accountants, we naturally analyse everything and then analyse it again to be sure. There's no 80/20 for us, it's 100% or nothing.

Challenge yourself and just start. It won't be perfect but you'll have started.

That's pretty much it. Easy, right? Start off nice and slowly at a pace that you're comfortable with. Get used to using the systems and talking about them to your existing clients and any new clients who walk through the door before you go creating massive marketing initiatives and launching it on the world, creating pressure for yourself and utilising precious time and money resources.

As accountants, we've practically made the word 'sales' taboo, the same as we have the word 'coach'. After reading this chapter, you may be thinking there's no way you can sell or even introduce clients to Business Metamorphosis®.

Yes, you can. Read *The Introvert's Edge* and remember that sales is just about five things, of which you have already nailed three by reading this book and doing the actions at the end of the chapters. The other two are your actions for this chapter so you are all sorted. If you're struggling with your strategic foundation, your PLAN, I'm very happy for you to use my Big Hairy Audacious Goal, 'reverse global business failure rates', to get you started.

'My team isn't interested in doing any of this, it's just me.'

And that's okay. Start with just you as you work through The Small Business Project. Team engagement will increase. They will soon see your successes and want a ticket to ride.

'I've never held a client information night before. It sounds a bit daunting and complicated to organise.'

As I said, keep it simple and small. Invite 25 and you may have five or 10 accept. Have some drinks and nibbles afterwards to keep it relaxed and give everyone an opportunity to talk to you if they want to. Remember: have one of the team ready to book DISCOVER meetings/calls on the spot.

And that's a wrap. Thank you so much for taking the time to read *Accounting Revolution*, how to instantly connect with clients in a way that makes you money. I hope you have enjoyed it and have taken loads of information and great ideas from it. I'd love to hear your comments and feedback so hit me up on any of my socials. I love reading all the comments. Over and out for now.

Actions to Take After Reading This Chapter

1. Schedule time in your calendar to work on your sales messaging.

2. Schedule regular team meetings.

3. Practice storytelling in team meetings.

4. Set a goal to introduce Business Metamorphosis® to three clients per week.

5. Set a goal to book one DISCOVER meeting/call per month.

6. Set a date for a client information night in approximately eight weeks.

Additional Information/Resources

- BM Introduction Script (Chapter 2 Business Metamorphosis®)

- Client Information Night Checklist.

You will find the links to download all the documents listed under the above two headings here: https://lyndasteffens.com/bonuses

Afterword

Congratulations! Well done for reading right to the end of the book, where few people have ventured. And even better if you've followed through with all the actions at the end of the chapters. You will be well on your way to changing your conversations and doing more of the work you and your team love.

Embracing The Coach Approach is the smartest thing you can do for your clients, your team, your business, your personal professional development, your family, and your life. I know once you've dipped your toe in the water, you'll see the light and never go back to trying to deliver advisory services using an expert mindset. It doesn't work and it's no fun. Go forth and coach, it's taboo no more!

It's been an absolute pleasure to bring all this information to you and if I have missed anything, I expect an email. I would love to give you the answers and help you out on this journey. Feel free to follow me on Facebook, connect with me on LinkedIn, or come chat to me at my events and when I'm out and about speaking. Share with me your stories. I love hearing them and it gives me more storytelling material to help other accountants learn how important it is to change their conversations, connect with their clients, and change lives.

You might have skimmed over a chapter or two and not quite got to do all the actions. Go back and reread one chapter a week, working through the actions. That's just 12 weeks, and what's 90 days in the big scheme of things? It's not a long time. In 90 days, your life can change. Your business most certainly will.

I regularly network and speak with people in small businesses. They all tell me they want better relationships with their accountants. A relationship where they feel comfortable sitting and discussing the trials and tribulations of business, and about what keeps them up at night and what they can do about it. They recognise their accountant knows heaps of cool stuff about business that they don't know themselves, and that this information could help smooth their business journey. But they are a little daunted by us, a little scared of looking silly and asking dumb questions. Business owners don't know what they don't know and they realise they don't know the right questions to ask. So, it's up to you to ask the questions. You know all the right questions. I've given them to you. Asking questions will connect you with your clients in a way they will value and that allows you to help them so much more. Come on, just do it!

I've been hanging out with accountants for a long time now and it never gets old seeing someone take the initial daunting step of trying something different, then realising almost instantly that it works, it's fabulous, and they want to try doing it again. Changing lives is at the true core of why I do what I do and hearing the words 'thank you' and 'thank you for saving my business', 'thank you for changing my life', makes my heart sing. Together we can change the lives of many more people in small businesses for the better. Small business is the lifeblood of our families, our schools, our communities, our economies, and our lives. Let's all do what we can.

If you had said to me just 12 months ago I was going to write and publish a book, I would have told you that you were crazy, that there was no way I could do that. But here it is and if I can write a book and share it with the world, then you can change your conversations. It's all about focusing on the big picture, your why. My book will change the landscape of accounting forever and it's just the first part of my vision for The Small Business Project. Stay tuned. You don't want to miss what I have in store for you.

So congratulations once again. I'm very proud of you for having reached this part of the book. I can't wait to hear about your journey. I'm here and waiting.

Cheers for now.

References

AZ Quotes 2019, *Quotes by Lisa Stone*, viewed 7 August 2019
https://www.azquotes.com/author/71951-Lisa_Stone

AZ Quotes 2019, *500 Quotes by Peter Drucker*, viewed 7 August 2019,
https://www.azquotes.com/author/4147-Peter_Drucker?p=4

Addicted2Success 2019, *38 Memorable Henry Ford Quotes*, viewed 8 August 2019,
https://addicted2success.com/quotes/38-memorable-henry-ford-quotes

BrainyMedia Inc 2019, *Gary Ryan Blair Quotes – BrainyQuote*, viewed 7 August
2019, https://www.brainyquote.com/authors/gary-ryan-blair-quotes

BrainyMedia Inc 2019, *Maya Angelou Quotes – BrainyQuote*, viewed 8 August
2019 https://www.brainyquote.com/authors/maya-angelou-quotes

BrainyMedia Inc 2019, *Top 10 Isaac Newton Quotes*, viewed 8 August 2019,
https://www.brainyquote.com/lists/authors/top-10-isaac-newton-quotes

Collins J, Porras J 2005, *Built to Last*, Random House, London

Covey S R 2013, *The 7 habits of highly effective people*, RosettaBooks, New York

Dolan G 2017, *Stories for work*, John Wiley & Sons Australia, Brisbane

Ferriss T 2009, *The 4-hour work week*, Harmony, London

Goodman E 2016, *Forbes Book of Quotes: 10,000 Thoughts on the Business of Life*,
Black Dog & Leventhal, New York

Goalcast Inc 2019, *Top 20 Simon Sinek Quotes That Reveal the Hard Truths About
Success*, viewed 8 August 2019, https://www.goalcast.com/2017/08/29/top-simon-
sinek-quotes-hard-truths-success

Goodreads Inc 2019, *A quote by Antoine de Saint-Exupéry.*, viewed 8 August 2019,
https://www.goodreads.com/quotes/87476-a-goal-without-a-plan-is-just-a-wish

Goodreads Inc 2019, *A quote by Larry Page*, viewed 7 August 2019,
https://www.goodreads.com/quotes/4101529-always-deliver-more-than-expected

Goodreads Inc 2019, *Charles W. Colson Quotes (Author of Born Again)*, viewed 7 August 2019,
https://www.goodreads.com/author/quotes/27694.Charles_W_Colson

Goodreads Inc 2019, *Marilyn Vos Savant Quotes (Author of Brain Building in Just 12 Weeks)*, viewed 7 August 2019,
https://www.goodreads.com/author/quotes/44295.Marilyn_Vos_Savant

Goodreads Inc 2019, *W. Edwards Deming Quotes (Author of Out of the Crisis)*, viewed 7 August 2019,
https://www.goodreads.com/author/quotes/310261.W_Edwards_Deming

Goodreads Inc 2019, *Endale Edith Quotes*, viewed 7 August 2019,
https://www.goodreads.com/author/quotes/18003431.Endale_Edith

Goulston, M 2010, *Just Listen: Discover the Secret to Getting Through to Absolutely Anyone,* AMACON, sourced through Soundview Executive Book Summaries, Concordville, Pa

Hinge Research Institute 2018, *2018 High Growth Study: Accounting & Financial Services Edition | Executive Summary*

Hoagland-Smith L 2019, *Prescription Without Diagnosis Is Malpractice*, viewed 8 August 2019 http://processspecialist.com/increasesales/executive-coaching/prescription-without-diagnosis-malpractice

https://www.leonardodavinci.net. (2019). *Leonardo da Vinci's Famous Quotes.* [online] Available at:
https://www.leonardodavinci.net/quotes.jsp [Accessed 8 Aug. 2019].

Hood, B 2019, *The profession's biggest challenges*, viewed 8 August 2019, https://www.accountingtoday.com/news/the-accounting-professions-biggest-challenges/

Hutyra, H 2019, *119 Socrates Quotes That Offer A More Peaceful Way Of Life,* viewed 8 August 2019, https://www.keepinspiring.me/socrates-quotes/

Inspirational Quotes 2018. *Michael John Bobak Quotes,* viewed 7 August 2019, http://inspiquotes.com/authors/michael-john-bobak-quotes/

Mindshop 2019, *Mindshop 2019 Business Advisory Report*, viewed 8 August 2019, https://www.wwaustralasia.com/wp-content/uploads/2019/02/Mindshop-Business-Advisory-Insights-for-Success-2019.pdf

Musashi, M 2002, *A Book of Five Rings & The Unfettered Mind*, translated from Japanese by Harris, V, Axiom, Australia.

NAB 2018, *Key Insights into the Australian Accounting Industry*, viewed 8 August 2019, https://business.nab.com.au/wp-content/uploads/2018/02j002905-Professional-Services-Insights-Report_v5.pdf/

Pollard, M 2018, *The Introvert's Edge: How the Quiet and Shy Can Outsell Anyone*, AMACOM.

Smith, R 2015, *The Best Time to Plant a Tree Was 20 Years Ago, No Matter*, *viewed 8 August 2019*, https://www.psychologytoday.com/us/blog/joy-and-pain/201504/the-best-time-plant-tree-was-20-years-ago-no-matter

STANDS4 2001- 2019, *Famous Quotes by: Spiderman*, viewed 8 August 2019, https://www.quotes.net/authors/Spider-Man

Valente, C 2006, *The Orphan's Tales: In the night garden*, Spectre, New York.

About the Author

Lynda Steffens, B.Bus CPA JP (Qual) SMJ Master Coach

Founder of The Small Business Project, a three-phase program that incorporates Business Metamorphosis®, Leading Edge Business™ and Ready Set Coach™ workshops and programs, Lynda has more than 25 years' experience in the professional services industry as an accountant, business advisor, partner, practice manager, speaker, and coach. She exclusively coaches accountants, revolutionising the way they engage with their clients, resulting in highly valued outcomes for their businesses. Her number one goal is to reignite their passion for being in business and show them that small changes can make big differences. With passion and motivation, people can do and create anything.

Born into business, she grew up on the family farm in the Lockyer Valley, a regional farming community in Queensland, Australia. Her career has seen her work with and advise countless SME business owners, helping them through the highs and lows, travelling with them on their business journey.

Having owned three businesses of her own, Lynda's business knowledge is extensive and her passion evident.

Inquisitive and passionate about people and their uniqueness, she sees no limit to what people with different strengths and perspectives can create together. An instinctive gatherer of information, a collector of interesting factoids, articles, and insights, she always has something practical in her toolbox that helps people make sense of the situation and solve their problem.

Lynda lives and breathes accounting and is passionate about the industry that has shaped her career. She enjoys working with the people in the profession.

Her vision for the future is one where accountants and the accounting industry play a vital role in the success of small businesses globally. A future where accountants are recognised as the most valuable and reliable source of business knowledge and expertise, where business success rates, not business failure rates, are the norm that are celebrated and talked about.

Always generous with her knowledge, optimistic, and with a contagious energy, she is a quintessential speaker and coach.

Check out Lynda's website https://lyndasteffens.com for her latest news, blogs, and workshops, or drop her a line at hello@lyndasteffens.com

Programs and Offers

Offer 1 – Advisory Unpack Session

Not sure what advisory means to you? Need a little help to get those advisory juices flowing?

Do you already offer advisory services but don't quite know how to organise them?

Are you ready to build your advisory service model, delivering regular and consistent advisory services and building the advisory practice of your dreams?

Get all the inspiration you need with our Advisory Unpack. We step you through unpacking your advisory services and slotting them into the Leading Edge Business™ program.

It takes about 45 minutes to work through this with you and map out your own 5Ps.

You walk away with:

- Your 5Ps advisory service map
- Advisory services that meet 5P's objectives
- Advisory service product build template
- Clarity around advisory service pricing
- Your fully formed Leading Edge Business™ program.

This package alone will change the way you view advisory services.

Total value: $597

Your investment: just $97

Email: book@lyndasteffens.com with subject line 'Advisory Unpack Offer' (mention you saw this offer in this book).

Do it now. Sometimes later becomes never! – Anonymous.

Offer 2 – Mini 3Ds Q & A Session

DISCOVER DIG DELIVER

Got questions about DISCOVER, DIG or DELIVER?

Not sure you've quite got the gist of the 3Ds process?

Are you ready to launch into the 3Ds but just need a little clarification and guidance?

Normally only offered to our 'Revolutionise' members, this session is just too good not to share.

Spend 30 minutes getting the answers and clarity to achieve the confidence you need to tackle the 3Ds like a pro.

This session will have you walking away with newfound confidence and assurance.

Total value: $297

Your investment: just $47

Email: book@lyndasteffens.com with subject line 'Mini 3Ds Q & A Offer' (mention you saw this offer in this book).

Well begun is half done — Aristotle

Offer 3 – The Small Business Project Certification

Want to Join the Revolution?

Become a TSBP Certified Advisor.

Here's what's on offer:

The Small Business Project Program	Restore	Revamp	Revolutionise
Business Metamorphosis ®			
Three (3) Day Workshop incl all workbooks & materials	X	X	X
Business Metamorphosis® Model (PDF)	X	X	X
Business Metamorphosis® Interactive Model (PDF)	X	X	X
Business Metamorphosis® Model Graphic Poster (A4)		X	X
Business Metamorphosis® Model Graphic Poster (A3)		X	X
Business Metamorphosis Model® Graphic Poster (A2)			X
The 3Ds ™ Implementation Tools			
DISCOVER Session Critiques*	1x	2x	3x
Basic DIG Package Review*		X	X
DELIVER Coaching Session**			X
The 3Ds™ Question & Answer Session**			X
Leading Edge Business ™			
Three (3) Day Workshop incl all workbooks & materials	X	X	X
Leading Edge Business™ Model (PDF)	X	X	X
Leading Edge Business™ Model Poster (A4)		X	X
Leading Edge Business™ Model Poster (A3)		X	X
Leading Edge Business™ Model Poster (A2)			X
The 5Ps ™ Implementation Tools			
Advisory Unpack**	X	X	X
PLAN Meeting Debrief Sessions (30mins)*	1x	2x	3x
The Coach Approach - Master Class**			X
Advisory Service Product Build Workshop**			X
Ready Set Coach ™			
Module 1 - Strategic Foundation	X	X	X
Module 2 - Operational Excellence	X	X	X
Module 3 - Team Surveys	X	X	X
Module 4 - Team Retreat	X	X	Y
Module 5 - Upfront Pricing		X	X
Module 6 - Tax Planning			X
Module 7 - Optional Topic (100% Customisable)			X
Community, Knowledge & Support			
TSBP Closed Facebook Group Access	X	X	X
Website Member Only Access (12 months)		X	X
One on One Mentoring Support (3 months)*			X
Unlimited Phone and Email Support (12 months)			X
TSPB Certification			
Framed Certification Certificate			X
"TSPB Powered By" Logo for Website & Social Media			X
Bonuses			
Accounting Revolution Book			2x
Discounted Rates for Authentic Leadership Corporate Series			X
Discounted Rates on TSBP Events			X
Discounted Rate on our Referral Partner Events			
Got some questions?			
Email or talk to us today!			
Web: www.lyndasteffens.com Email: book@lyndasteffens.com			
*Sessions delivered via Phone			
** Sessions delivered via Zoom			

www.ingramcontent.com/pod-product-compliance
Lightning Source LLC
Chambersburg PA
CBHW071159210326
41597CB00016B/1602